AIR POLLUTION MANAGEMENT

AIR POLLUTION MANAGEMENT

Edited by
Dr. Rabi Narayana Misra
M.Com., LLB., M.Phil, Ph.D.

DPH

DISCOVERY PUBLISHING HOUSE PVT. LTD.
NEW DELHI-110 002

Published by:
Tilak Wasan
DISCOVERY PUBLISHING HOUSE PVT. LTD.
4383/4B, Ansari Road, Darya Ganj
New Delhi-110 002 (India)
Phone : +91-11-23279245, 43596064-65
Fax : +91-11-23253475
E-mail : discoverypublishinghouse@gmail.com
sales@discoverypublishinggroup.com
web : www.discoverypublishinggroup.com

First Edition: **2015**

ISBN: 978-93-5056-724-1

Air Pollution Management

Printed at:
Infinity Imaging Systems
Delhi

PREFACE

Air pollution is the introduction into the atmosphere of chemical particulates and biological matter that harm to human, other living organs and causes damage to the natural environment. Air pollution comes into picture due to the accumulation of hazardous substances into the atmosphere that causes danger to human life and other living matter.

Air is a part of the atmopshere which is present above the earth's surface. Actually air is a mechanical mixture of solid particles (dust and smoke) moisture naturally occurring chemical gases such as Nitrogen, Oxygen and traces of rare gases. Air is highly essential for the survival of all living beings on the earth as all living beings inhale the atmospheric air during the respiration. The loss of oxygen gas from the atmosphere is being usually compensated by the oxygen gas supplied from the trees and plants present in the nature. In fact all living beings inhale oxygen gas and exhale carbon dioxide gas during their respiration.

To live healthy, peacefully, stress free life, it need due consideration for pollution free environment mostly, air pollution free environment society. This book is very much helpful to the scholars, planners, engineers, general public, government, industrial sectors, and others who are dealing with environment.

Dr. R.N. Misra

ACKNOWLEDGEMENTS

I am very thankful to all paper contributors of this book. It is not possible on my part to edit this book without their active co-operation and help.

I am thankful to Smt. Swarnaprava Misra, President of Lions Club of Berhampur Gold (International) and other members of the Lions Club for organizing a National Seminar on Air Pollution Management on 9th Feb. 2014 and allowed me to publish the suitable articles in my edited book. I also convey my thanks to the Governor Lion Kalpana Biswal for her kind co-operation and help for conducting the National Seminar on Air Pollution on 09.02.2014.

I also convey my thanks and express my gratitude to Mr. Tilak Wasan, the Director of Discovery Publishing House (P) Ltd., New Delhi for publishing this book without hesitation. Further I am also thankful to his son Parul Wasan and Namit Wasan and other members of Discovery Publishing House (P) Ltd., New Delhi, for their kind help and co-operation for publishing this book in time.

Dr. R.N. Misra

CONTENTS

1

Transport Sector as Source of Air Pollution

(An Overview)

Dr. Santosh Kumar Badatya*
Dr. Rabi Narayan Misra**

Introduction

When something is added to the environment which is very harmful, poisonous for the living organs such as animal, people etc. is called pollution. In simple words, when environment not fit for the use is called pollution. Pollution not only affects to the human beings but also to others like plants, trees, and animals pets etc. The other effects of pollution are acid rain, ozone deflection, global climate changes, crops and forest damages etc. on environment. The major causes of pollution are industrial waste, commercial waste, agricultural waste, day-to-day human activities, mode of transport and many other sources. Pollution weak our ecosystem of earth. So should always to make our all efforts to control our waste and not to through it into the river, seas, land etc.

Air pollution is the introduction into the atmosphere of chemicals, particulates, and biological matter that harm to humans, other living organs or cause damage to the natural environment. Air pollution comes into picture due to the accumulation of hazardous substances into the atmosphere that danger human life and other living matter. The most dominant player responsible for automobiles, combustion of

* Sr. Faculty Member, MBA, SMIT, Ankushpur, Berhampur, Ganjam, Odisha.
** Professor, MBA, Gandhi Nagar-6th li, Berhampur, Ganjam, Odisha.

coal, acid rain, manufacturing of building, tobacco smoke, paint fumes, aerosol sprays, nuclear weapons and wild fires. The earth is capable of cleaning itself of a certain level of pollution, but man-made pollution have becomes too numerous for the earth's natural mechanisms to remove. As far as effect of air pollution is concerned, many diseases caused such as respiratory disease, heart disease, asthma, eye disease etc. due to air pollution. The second one is heart disease, it caused due to increased level of carbon monoxide in the air. The statistics shows that, this year air pollution segment will count for 80% of premature death.

Transport is widely recognized to be a significant and increasing source of air pollution worldwide. One of the main causes of air pollution is manufacturing industries. This source of pollution sweeps particulate matter and chemicals into the atmosphere. The exhaust from a factory includes sulphur oxides, nitrogen oxides, carbon monoxide and dioxide, as well as volatile organic compounds and particulates. There is not an area of the Earth's atmosphere organ ecosystem that has not been altered by the long-term effects of the pollution created by manufacturing. Strides have made to filthier the material coming from manufacturing plants, but it may take the Earth millennia to completely recover from the damage already done.

Objectives of the Study

1. The role of transport sector in Odisha in air pollution.
2. The various causes of air pollution.
3. The importance of air pollution.
4. The various effects of air pollution

Composition of Air

Air is invisible mixer of gases. It is made up mainly: 1. Nitrogen (78%) 2. Oxygen (21%). It also contains water vapour and small amounts of other gases. 3. Other gases include carbon dioxide, ozone helium and hydrogen among others.

Importance of Air

1. **Existing of Living Organs:** Air is most important for human beings, animal, plants etc. All living organs need oxygen in their existence in the environment. They take oxygen from the air in the process of breathing. This oxygen helps to produce energy from the food. In this process carbon dioxide is formed which is breathed out.
2. **Maintain a Balance:** Animal and human beings need oxygen from the air and give out carbon dioxide gas to the air. This carbon dioxide used by the plants at the time of photosynthesis and gives out oxygen. In this process nature maintain balance between carbon dioxide and oxygen.
3. **Role of Nitrogen:** Nitrogen gas also essential for the growth of plants. Plant cannot absorb directly from the air. This nitrogen gas is converted into nitrates and ammonium salts with the help of bacteria present in the soil. Plant absorbs these to form proteins which are essential for their growth.
4. **Act as Shield:** Atmosphere also acts as a shield like an umbrella to protect from the harmful rays of sunlight. Ozone gas which is present in the upper part of the atmosphere, prevent harmful ultraviolet rays of sunlight to reaching the surface of the earth. Thus, ozone layer protects the harmful effects of the ultraviolet rays present in the sunlight on animals and plants.

Types of Pollution

1. Air pollution
2. Water Pollution
3. Noise Pollution
4. Heat or light Pollution
5. Solid Pollution
6. Energy Pollution, etc.

Causes or Sources of Air Pollution

There are several main causes of air pollution; the vast majority of them can be attributed by man. The earth is capable of cleaning itself of a certain level of pollution, but man-made pollution have became too numerous for the Earth's natural mechanisms to remove. We are seeing the results of this overload in the form of acid rain, smog and the variety of health problems that can be contributed to our environment. Air pollution includes various causes such as:

1. Industrial waste
2. Agricultural waste
3. Commercial waste
4. Mode of Transportation
5. Due to dust storm
6. Crushing stones and quarries
7. Smokes from forest fire
8. Burning of coal in power houses
9. Burning of wood, cow dung and garbage
10. Germs from coughing and sneezing
11. Tobacco smokes
12. Nuclear weapons
13. Acid rains.

One of the main causes of air pollution is transport sector. A well-developed transport network and efficient communication system are basic prerequisite for rapid economic development and sustained growth. Traffic congestion is severe in India's cities and towns. It is caused for several reasons, some of which are: increase in number of vehicles per kilometre of available road, a lack of intra-city divided-lane highways and intra-city expressways networks, lack of inter-city expressways, traffic accidents and chaos from poor enforcement of traffic laws.

Transport Sector in Odisha

In Odisha, the State Transport Authority (STA) is the Apex body of motor vehicle department. It looks after the administration and management of road transport sector of the State. The air pollution is intimately connected to land-use and transportation. It includes such as community planning, road design, traffic control and mass transportation etc.

Traffic congestion reduces average traffic speed. At low speeds vehicle burns more fuels and pollute more per trip. At average trip speeds between 20 to 40 kilometres per hour, the cars pollutant emission was twice as much as when the average speed was 55 to 75 kilometres per hour. The fuel efficiencies similarly were much worse with traffic congestion.

Table 1.1 : Details of Different Number of Motor Vehicles on Road in Odisha for the Period from 2001-2011

Year	No of Buses	Good vehicles	Cars/ Taxies/ Jeeps	Moter Cycle/ Scooters	Three Whee-lers	Other Vehicles/ Tractors	Total Vehicles	% Incre-ases
2001	4499	67743	51979	735742	6167	NA	866150	—
2002	4787	77147	58670	826548	8787	NA	973939	12.44
2003	4946	84268	66691	943178	11310	NA	1110391	14.02
2004	5297	94859	80510	1064323	15086	11789	1271864	14.59
2005	5997	119352	95531	1208210	18811	13092	1460993	14.88
2006	6395	94130	114469	1368209	23610	60751	1667564	14.14
2007	6699	109738	136792	1537758	27314	66279	1884580	13.07
2008	6877	115108	140260	1691684	31700	89887	2070216	09.84
2009	7647	136174	152213	1870020	37784	103307	2307145	11.44
2010	8908	159881	164614	2132508	52873	120792	2639576	14.40
2011	12264	169032	189197	2453364	55364	154740	3033944	14.93

Sources: *Economic Survey 2010-11*, Directorate of Economics & Statistics, Government of Odisha, BBSR.

The growth of vehicles from 2001 to 2011 has been represented in Table 1.1. The total No. of vehicles was 8,66,150 in 2001, but it has grown to a level of 30,33,944 in 2011. It signifies the growth of vehicles 350 times during the study period. It is also found that the annual growth rate of vehicles on an average of 14 per cent in most of the year during the study period. The growth rate of vehicles is lowest (9.84%) in the year 2008 and highest (14.93%) in the year 2011. In the year 2010, the 80 per cent of total vehicles is under two wheelers and both car and goods vehicles is 6 per cent each. The automobiles emission is an environmental hazard in major cities in the State such as Bhubaneswar, Cuttack, Sambalpur, Berhampur, Rourkela etc. The State Government has taken Pollution Under Control (PUC) certificate obligatory for all categories of vehicles since 1997. As in 2008, 79 pollution testing centre have been opened by the Government to checkup auto emission levels and issue PUC certificate to different categories of vehicles. The other preventive measures have also taken by the Government like use gas analyzers, catalytic converters and use of unleaded petrol in two and four wheelers have been initiated by the Government to minimize the hazards of vehicles pollution.

Effects of Air Pollution

1. **Acid Rain:** When nitrogen dioxide and sulphur dioxide comes with rain water forms acid. This acid rain damage:

   (*i*) Agricultural Crops

   (*ii*) Reduces fertility of soil

   (*iii*) Damages monuments made of marbles.
2. Suffocation, cough, headache, skin and eye diseases
3. Greenhouse effects (Global Warming)
4. Heart Diseases
5. Respiratory diseases
6. Asthma.

Control of Air Pollution

Pollution weak the balance of our ecosystem of earth. So we should always to make efforts to control pollution by minimizing waste, and not throwing it to river, ocean and land. Some preventive steps should be taken to minimize air pollutions:

1. The Air Prevention and Control of Pollution Act was passed in 1981 to control pollution and measurable improvement.
2. In the period 2001-2010 supply of more electricity to urban and rural areas to control the burning of wood, cow dung and kerosene.
3. Supply of more LPG gases as domestic fuel instead of coal and fuel wood.
4. We should plant more trees to reduce the greenhouse effects and maintain the balance of temperature.
5. Lesser use of vehicles. We should go to the office by buses and sharing autos.
6. Regular checkup of vehicles.
7. Dumping the garbage in a pit to make it manure.
8. Construction of tall chimneys in power houses and factories.
9. Good habits of covering at the time of coughing and sneezing.

REFERENCES

Atmananda (2009), *Energy and Sustainable Development—An Indian Prospective*. World Academy of Science.

Economic Survey of Odisha 2011-12, Government of Odisha.

2

Air Pollution

(Impact on Human Health)

Dr. P. Divakara Rao*
Dr. R.N. Misra**

Introduction

The human health effects of poor air quality are far-reaching, but principally affect the body's respiratory system and the cardiovascular system. Individual reactions to air pollutants depend on the type of pollutant a person is exposed to, the degree of exposure, the individual's health status and genetics. People who exercise outdoors, for example, on hot, smoggy days increase their exposure to pollutants in the air.

The health effects caused by air pollutants may range from subtle biochemical and physiological changes to difficulty in breathing, wheezing, coughing and aggravation of existing respiratory and cardiac conditions. These effects can result in increased medication use, increased doctor or emergency room visits, more hospital admissions and even premature death.

Human Respiratory System

The health of our lungs and entire respiratory system is affected by the quality of the air we breathe. In addition to oxygen, this air contains other substances such as pollutants, which can be harmful. Exposure to chemicals by inhalation can negatively affect our lungs and other organs in the body.

---

* Lecturer in Commerce, Govt. Degree College, Tuni, East Dodavari District, Andhra Pradesh.

** Professor, MBA, Gandhi Nagar-6th li, Berhampur, Ganjam, Odisha.

The respiratory system is particularly sensitive to air pollutants because much of it is made up of exposed membrane. Lungs are anatomically structured to bring large quantities of air (on average, 400 million litres in a lifetime) into intimate contact with the blood system, to facilitate the delivery of oxygen.

Lung tissue cells can be injured directly by air pollutants such as ozone, metals and free radicals. Ozone can damage the alveoli—the individual air sacs in the lung where oxygen and carbon dioxide are exchanged. More specifically, airway tissues which are rich in bioactivation enzymes can transform organic pollutants into reactive metabolites and cause secondary lung injury. Lung tissue has an abundant blood supply that can carry toxic substances and their metabolites to distant organs. In response to toxic insult, lung cells also release a variety of potent chemical mediators that may critically affect the function of other organs such as those of the cardiovascular system. This response may also cause lung inflammation and impair lung function.

Structure and Function

The human respiratory system is dominated by our lungs, which bring fresh oxygen (O_2) into our bodies while expelling carbon dioxide (CO_2). The oxygen travels from the lungs through the bloodstream to the cells in all parts of the body. The cells use the oxygen as fuel and give off carbon dioxide as a waste gas. The waste gas is carried by the bloodstream back to the lungs to be exhaled.

The lungs accomplish this vital process - called gas exchange - using an automatic and quickly adjusting control system. This gas exchange process occurs in conjunction with the central nervous system (CNS), the circulatory system, and the musculature of the diaphragm and the chest.

The human respiratory system can be divided into the upper respiratory tract and the lower respiratory tract. The upper respiratory tract includes the following rigid structures:

- **Nasal cavities:** Filter the air we breathe and provide a sense of smell.
- **Pharynx:** Acts in the respiratory and the digestive system.
- **Larynx:** Link between the pharynx and the trachea. Generates the voice with the presence of vocal folds.
- **Trachea:** The trachea is the bond with the lower respiratory tract. This is a flexible structure allowing the air to go down to the lungs.

In addition to gas exchange, the lungs and the other parts of the respiratory system have important jobs to do related to breathing. These include:

- Bringing all air to the proper body temperature.
- Moisturizing the inhaled air for necessary humidity.
- Protecting the body from harmful substances by coughing, sneezing, filtering or swallowing them, or by alerting the body through the sense of smell.

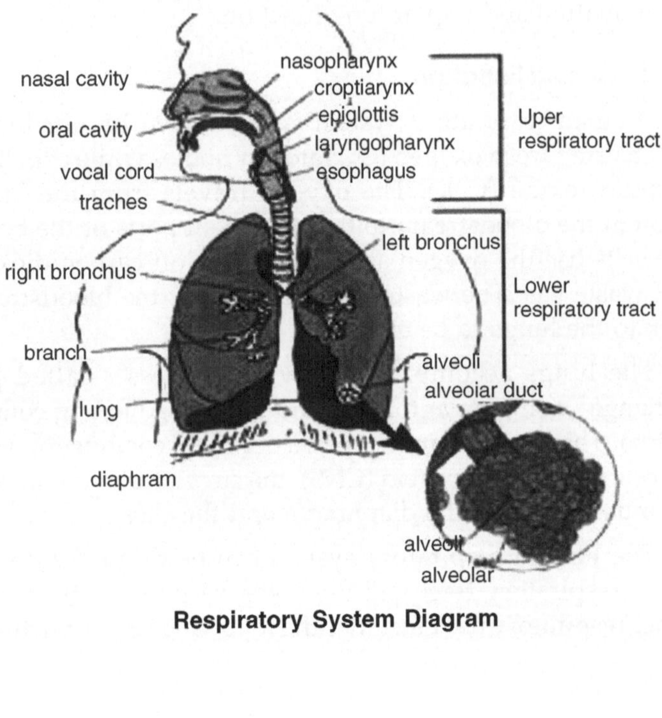

Respiratory System Diagram

- Defending the lungs with cilia (tiny hair-like structure), mucus and macrophages, which act to remove harmful substances deposited in the respiratory system.

The respiratory system is sensitive to air pollution. The cardiovascular system can be affected as well.

Human Cardiovascular System

The cardiovascular system has two major components: the heart and a network of blood vessels. The cardiovascular system supplies the tissues and cells of the body with nutrients, respiratory gases, hormones, and metabolites and removes the waste products of cellular metabolism as well as foreign matter. It is also responsible for maintaining the optimal internal homeostasis of the body and the critical regulation of body temperature and pH.

The inhalation of air pollutants eventually leads to their absorption into the bloodstream and transport to the heart. A wide spectrum of chemical and biological substances may interact directly with the cardiovascular system to cause structural changes, such as degenerative necrosis and inflammatory reactions. Some pollutants may also directly cause functional alterations that affect the rhythmicity and contractility of the heart. If severe enough, functional changes may lead to lethal arrhythmias without major evidence of structural damage to the myocardium.

There also may be indirect actions secondary to changes in other organ systems, especially the central and autonomic nervous systems and selective actions of the endocrine system. Some cytokins released from other inflamed organs may also produce adverse cardiovascular effects, such as reducing the mechanical performance and metabolic efficiency of the heart and blood vessels.

Many chemical substances may cause the formation of reactive oxygen. This oxidative metabolism is considered to be critical to the preservation of cardiovascular function. For example, oxygen free radicals oxidize low-density lipoproteins, and this reaction is thought to be involved in the formation of the atherosclerotic plaques. Oxidized low-density lipoproteins can injure blood vessel cells and increase adherence and the migration of inflammatory cells to the injured area. The production of oxygen free radicals in heart tissues have been associated with arrhythmias, and heart cell death.

Heart and Lung Diseases

Heart and lung illnesses and diseases are common in Canada, and there are many factors that can increase the chances of contracting them such as smoking and genetic predisposition. The role of air pollution as the underlying cause remains unclear but is the subject of considerable research. However, it is clear that air pollution, infections and allergies can exacerbate these conditions. An early diagnosis can lead to appropriate treatment and ensure a normal or close to normal quality of life. In many cases however, there is no cure and those affected may die prematurely. The following are the most prevalent diseases:

- **Minor Lung Illnesses**-The common cold is the most familiar of these, with symptoms including sore throat, stuffy or runny nose, coughing and sometimes irritation of the eyes.
- **Lung Infections**-croup, bronchitis, and pneumonia are caused by viruses or bacteria and are very common. Symptoms may include cough, fever, chills and shortness of breath.
- **Asthma**-is an increasingly common chronic disease among children and adults. It causes shortness of breath, coughing or wheezing or whistling in the chest. Asthma attacks can be triggered by a variety of factors including exercise, infection, pollen, allergies and stress. It can also be triggered by a sensitivity to non-allergic types of pollutants present in the air such as smog.

- **Chronic Obstructive Pulmonary Disease (COPD)**-is also known as chronic obstructive lung disease and encompasses two major disorders: emphysema and chronic bronchitis. Emphysema is a chronic disorder in which the walls and elasticity of the alveoli are damaged. Chronic bronchitis is characterized by inflammation of the cells lining the inside of bronchi, which increases the risk of infection and obstructs airflow in and out of the lung. Smoking is responsible for approximately 80% of COPD cases while other forms of air pollution may also influence the development of these diseases. Symptoms include cough, production of mucous and shortness of breath. It is important to note that no cure exists for people suffering from COPD although healthy lifestyle and appropriate medication can help.
- **Lung Cancer**-is the most common cause of death due to cancer in women and men. Cigarette smoke contains various carcinogens and is responsible for most cases of this often fatal disease. The symptoms of lung cancer begin silently and then progress to chronic cough, wheezing and chest pain. Air pollution has been linked somewhat weakly to lung cancer.
- **Coronary Artery Disease** - refers to the narrowing or blocking of the arteries or blood vessels that supply blood to the heart. This disease includes angina and heart attack which share similar symptoms of pain or pressure in the chest. Unlike angina, the symptoms caused by heart attack do not subside with rest and may cause permanent damage to the heart. Smoking, lack of exercise, excess weight, high cholesterol levels in the blood, family history and high blood pressure are some of the factors that may contribute to this disease.
- **Heart Failure** - is a condition in which the heart is unable to cope with its work load of pumping blood to the lungs and the rest of the body. The most common cause

is severe coronary artery disease. The main symptoms are shortness of breath and swelling of the ankles and feet.

- **Heart-Rhythm Problems** - are irregular or abnormal rhythms of the heart beat. In some cases heart-rhythm problems are caused by coronary artery disease. Symptoms of heart-rhythm problems influttering in the chest (palpitation) and feeling light-headed. Some heart-rhythm problems are life-threatening and need emergency treatment.

Pyramid of Health Effects

Air pollution can affect both the respiratory and cardiac systems. The health effects of air pollution can be seen as a pyramid, with the mildest but not common effects at the bottom of the pyramid, and the least common but more severe at the top of the pyramid. The pyramid demonstrates that as severity decreases the number of people affected increases.

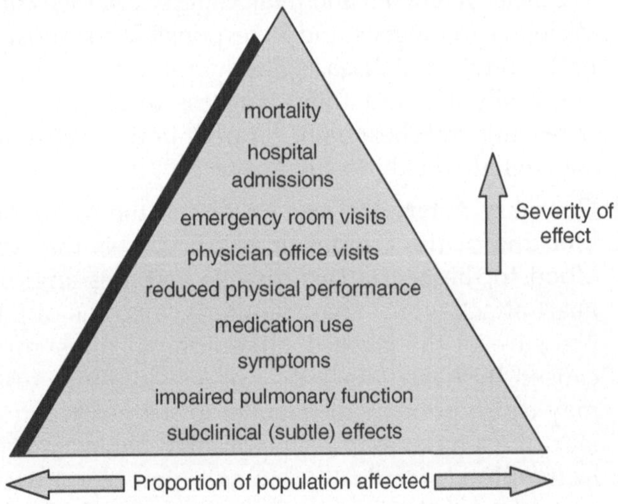

Health Endpoints Associated with Increased Air Pollutant Levels

- **Mortality:** All non-accidental mortality causes
- **Hospital Admissions:** Cardiovascular and Respiratory Hospital Admissions.

- **Emergency Room Visits:** Visit to an emergency department.
- **Asthma Symptom Days:** Exacerbation of asthma symptoms in individuals with diagnosed asthma.
- **Restricted Activity Days:** Days spent in bed, missed from work, and days when activities are partially restricted due to illness.
- **Acute Respiratory Symptoms:** Respiratory-related symptoms such as chest discomfort, coughing and wheezing.

Population at Risk

Although everyone is at risk from the health effects of air pollution, certain sub-populations are more susceptible. Individual reactions to air contaminants depend on several factors such as the type of pollutant, the degree of exposure and how much of the pollutant is present. Age and health are also important factors.

The elderly and people suffering from cardio-respiratory problems such as asthma appear to be the most susceptible groups.

Children and newborns are also sensitive to the health effects of air pollution since they take in more air than adults for their body weight and consequently, a higher level of pollutants. People who exercise outdoors on hot and smoggy days are also at greater risk due to their increased exposure to pollutants in the air.

Leading Causes of Hospitalization

Respiratory and cardiovascular diseases are among the leading causes of hospitalization in Canada. In 1996-1997 there were 3.16 million hospital admissions in Canada of which cardiovascular and respiratory diseases accounted for 15 per cent and 9 per cent, respectively.

Air pollution exacerbates the condition of people with respiratory and cardiovascular diseases and causes measurable increases in the rates of hospitalization for these diseases.

(Total Number of hospitalizations: 81,68,799, **Source:** Statistics Canada. 1999)

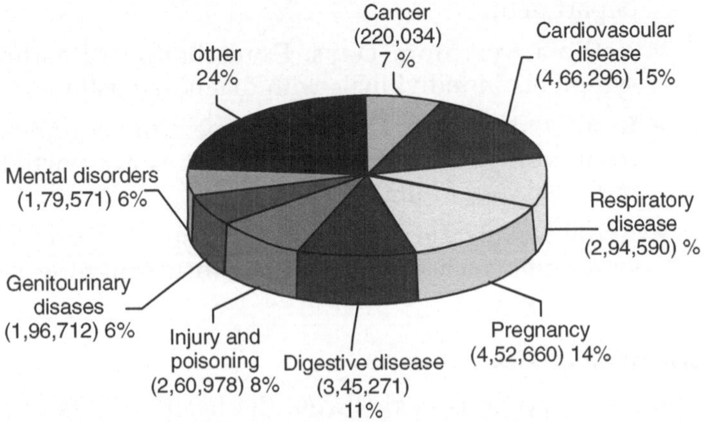

Leading Causes of Hospitalization Number and Percentage of Separation by Subgroup Canada 96-97

We do not yet understand the role of air pollution in causing these illnesses in the Canadian population.

Leading Causes of Death

Leading Causes of Death

(Total number of deaths in 1997: 2,15,669; **Source:** Statistics Canada, 1999)

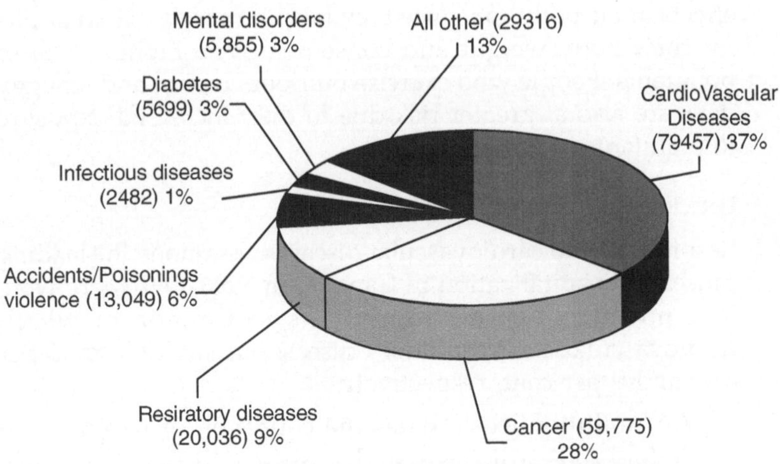

Number and Percentage of Deaths, Canada 1997

Cardiovascular and respiratory diseases are among the leading causes of death in Canada. In 1997, 37 per cent and 9 per cent of over 2,00,000 deaths were related to cardiovascular and respiratory diseases respectively.

Air pollution causes measurable increases in non-accidental mortality.

Estimating Health Benefits

When examining a specific pollution-reduction option (such as changing gasoline composition) regulators may estimate the reduction in health effects that are expected, and the value to society of avoiding those health problems.

As a society, we pay for the health effects of air pollution in many ways. Additional health care costs for the treatment of these effects may come from any of the following: hospital admissions, visits to the emergency room or doctor's office, homecare service, medication such as inhalers for asthma. Other considerations include lost productivity in the workplace, lost wages due to sick time, out of pocket expenses incurred while ill (e.g., additional child care costs), and, finally lost quality of life or life itself.

Value of Health Benefits

A recent study examined the economic value of reducing the health effects of air pollution by introducing cleaner vehicles and fuels in Canada. This study found that the economic value of avoiding these health effects was $24 billion over a period of 24 years, compared to a cost of $6 billion to implement the programme. This methodology has been used by Health Canada and Environment Canada in a number of initiatives to examine the benefits of control measures.

3

Air Pollution Management

Rachna Padhy*

Introduction

Air pollution management aims at the elimination, or reduction to acceptable levels, of airborne gaseous pollutants, suspended particulate matter and physical and, to a certain extent, biological agents whose presence in the atmosphere can cause adverse effects on human health (*e.g.*, irritation/ increase of incidence or prevalence of respiratory diseases, morbidity, cancer, excess mortality) or welfare (*e.g.*, sensory effects, reduction of visibility), deleterious effects on animal or plant life, damage to materials of economic value to society and damage to the environment (*e.g.*, climatic modifications). The serious hazards associated with radioactive pollutants, as well as the special procedures required for their control and disposal, also deserve careful attention.

The importance of efficient management of outdoor and indoor air pollution cannot be overemphasized. Unless there is adequate control, the multiplication of pollution sources in the modern world may lead to irreparable damage to the environment and mankind.

The objective of this article is to give a general overview of the possible approaches to the management of ambient air pollution from motor vehicle and industrial sources. However, it is to be emphasized from the very beginning that indoor

---

* Reader in English, K.K. College (Auto), Berhampur-1, Odisha.

air pollution (in particular, in developing countries) might play an even larger role than outdoor air pollution due to the observation that indoor air pollutant concentrations are often substantially higher than outdoor concentrations.

Beyond considerations of emissions from fixed or mobile sources, air pollution management involves consideration of additional factors (such as topography and meteorology, and community and government participation, among many others) all of which must be integrated into a comprehensive programme. For example, meteorological conditions can greatly affect the ground-level concentrations resulting from the same pollutant emission. Air pollution sources may be scattered over a community or a region and their effects may be felt by, or their control may involve, more than one administration. Furthermore, air pollution does not respect any boundaries, and emissions from one region may induce effects in another region by long-distance transport.

Air pollution management, therefore, requires a multidisciplinary approach as well as a joint effort by private and governmental entities.

Sources of Air Pollution

The sources of man-made air pollution (or emission sources) are of basically two types:

- *stationary,* which can be subdivided into area sources such as agricultural production, mining and quarrying, industrial, point and area sources such as manufacturing of chemicals, non-metallic mineral products, basic metal industries, power generation and community sources (*e.g.,* heating of homes and buildings, municipal waste and sewage sludge incinerators, fireplaces, cooking facilities, laundry services and cleaning plants)
- *mobile,* comprising any form of combustion-engine vehicles (*e.g.,* light-duty gasoline powered cars, light- and heavy-duty diesel powered vehicles, motorcycles, aircraft, including line sources with emissions of gases and particulate matter from vehicle traffic).

In addition, there are also natural sources of pollution (*e.g.*, eroded areas, volcanoes, certain plants which release great amounts of pollen, sources of bacteria, spores and viruses). Natural sources are not discussed in this article.

Types of Air Pollutants

Air pollutants are usually classified into suspended particulate matter (dusts, fumes, mists, smokes), gaseous pollutants (gases and vapours) and odours. Some examples of usual pollutants are presented below:

- *Suspended Particulate Matter (SPM, PM-10)* includes diesel exhaust, coal fly-ash, mineral dusts (*e.g.*, coal, asbestos, limestone, cement), metal dusts and fumes (*e.g.*, zinc, copper, iron, lead) and acid mists (*e.g.*, sulphuric acid), fluorides, paint pigments, pesticide mists, carbon black and oil smoke. Suspended particulate pollutants, besides their effects of provoking respiratory diseases, cancers, corrosion, destruction of plant life and so on, can also constitute a nuisance (*e.g.*, accumulation of dirt), interfere with sunlight (*e.g.*, formation of smog and haze due to light scattering) and act as catalytic surfaces for reaction of adsorbed chemicals.
- *Gaseous pollutants* include sulphur compounds [*e.g.*, sulphur dioxide (SO_2) and sulphur trioxide (SO_3)], carbon monoxide, nitrogen compounds [*e.g.*, nitric oxide (NO)], nitrogen dioxide (NO_2), ammonia], organic compounds (*e.g.*, hydrocarbons (HC), volatile organic compounds (VOC), polycyclic aromatic hydrocarbons (PAH), aldehydes), halogen compounds and halogen derivatives (*e.g.*, HF and HCl), hydrogen sulphide, carbon disulphide and mercaptans (odours).

Secondary pollutants may be formed by thermal, chemical or photochemical reactions. For example, by thermal action sulphur dioxide can oxidize to sulphur trioxide which, dissolved in water, gives rise to the formation of sulphuric acid mist (catalysed by manganese and iron oxides). Photochemical reactions between nitrogen oxides and reactive hydrocarbons can produce ozone (CO_3), formaldehyde and peroxyacetyl nitrate (PAN); reactions between HCl and formaldehyde can form bis-chloromethyl ether.

While some *odours* are known to be caused by specific chemical agents such as hydrogen sulphide (H_2S), carbon disulphide (CS_2) and mercaptans (R-SH or RI-S-R2) others are difficult to define chemically.

Examples of the main pollutants associated with some industrial air pollution sources are presented in Table 3.1 (Economopoulos 1993).

Table 3.1. Common Atmospheric Pollutants and their Sources

Category	Source
Agriculture	Open burning
Mining and quarrying	Coal mining Crude petroleum and natural gas production Non-ferrous ore mining Stone quarrying
Manufacturing	Food, beverages and tobacco Textiles and leather industries Wood products Paper products, printing
Manufacture of chemicals	Phthalic anhydride Chlor-alkali Hydrochloric acid Hydrofluoric acid Sulphuric acid Nitric acid Phosphoric acid Lead oxide and pigments Ammonia Sodium carbonate Calcium carbide Adipic acid Alkyl lead Maleic anhydride and terephthalic acid Fertilizer and pesticide production

Category	Source
	Ammonium nitrate Ammonium sulphate Synthetic resins, plastic materials, fibres Paints, varnishes, lacquers Soap Carbon black and printing ink Trinitrotoluene
Petroleum refineries	Miscellaneous products of petroleum and coal
Non-metallic mineral products manufacture	Glass products Structural clay products Cement, lime and plaster
Basic metal industries	Iron and steel Non-ferrous industries
Power generation	Electricity, gas and steam
Wholesale and retail trade	Fuel storage, filling operations
Transport	
Community services	Municipal incinerators

Source: Economopoulos 1993

Clean Air Implementation Plans (Air Quality Management)

Air quality management aims at the preservation of environmental quality by prescribing the tolerated degree of pollution, leaving it to the local authorities and polluters to devise and implement actions to ensure that this degree of pollution will not be exceeded. An example of legislation within this approach is the adoption of ambient air quality standards based, very often, on air quality guidelines for different pollutants; these are accepted maximum levels of pollutants (or indicators) in the target area (*e.g.*, at ground level at a specified point in a community) and can be either primary or secondary standards. Primary standards are the maximum levels consistent with an adequate safety margin and with the preservation of public health, and must be complied with within a specific time limit; secondary standards are those judged to be necessary for protection against known or anticipated adverse effects other than health hazards (mainly on vegetation) and must be complied "within a reasonable time". Air quality standards are short-, medium- or long-term values valid for 24 hours per day, 7 days per week, and for monthly, seasonal or annual exposure of all living subjects (including sensitive subgroups such as children, the elderly and the sick) as well as non-living objects; this is in contrast to maximum permissible levels for occupational exposure, which are for a partial weekly exposure (*e.g.*, 8 hours per day, 5 days per week) of adult and supposedly healthy workers.

Typical measures in air quality management are control measures at the source, for example, enforcement of the use of catalytic converters in vehicles or of emission standards in incinerators, land-use planning and shut-down of factories or reduction of traffic during unfavourable weather conditions. The best air quality management stresses that the air pollutant emission should be kept to a minimum; this is basically defined through emission standards for single sources of air pollution and could be achieved for industrial sources, for example, through closed systems and high-efficiency collectors. An emission standard is a limit on the amount or concentration of a pollutant. Motor vehicle emissions are controlled by controlling emissions per vehicle mile travelled (VMT) and by controlling VMT itself. Emissions per VMT can be reduced by controlling vehicle performance - hardware, maintenance - for both new and in-use cars. Fuel composition of leaded gasoline may be controlled by reducing lead or sulphur content, which also has a beneficial effect on decreasing HC emissions from vehicles. Lowering the levels of sulphur in diesel fuel as a means to lower diesel particulate emission has the additional beneficial effect of increasing the potential for catalytic control of diesel particulate and organic HC emissions.

Another important management tool for reducing vehicle evaporative and refuelling emissions is the control of gasoline volatility. Control of fuel volatility can greatly lower vehicle evaporative HC emissions. Use of oxygenated additives in gasoline lowers HC and CO exhaust as long as fuel volatility is not increased.

Reduction of VMT is an additional means of controlling vehicle emissions by control strategies such as :

- use of more efficient transportation modes
- increasing the average number of passengers per car
- spreading congested peak traffic loads
- reducing travel demand.

While such approaches promote fuel conservation, they are not yet accepted by the general population, and governments have not seriously tried to implement them.

All these technological and political solutions to the motor vehicle problem except substitution of electrical cars are increasingly offset by growth in the vehicle population. The vehicle problem can be solved only if the growth problem is addressed in an appropriate way.

Transportation and Land-Use Planning

The pollution problem is intimately connected to land-use and transportation, including issues such as community planning road design, traffic control and mass transportation; to concerns of demography, topography and economy; and to social concerns. In general, the rapidly growing urban aggregations have severe pollution problems due to poor land-use and transportation practices. Transportation planning for air pollution control includes transportation controls, transportation policies, mass transit and highway congestion costs. Transportation controls have an important impact on the general public in terms of equity, repressiveness and social and economic disruption - in particular, direct transportation controls such as motor vehicle constraints, gasoline limitations and motor vehicle emission reductions. Emission reductions due to direct controls can be reliably estimated and verified. Indirect transportation controls such as reduction of vehicle miles travelled by improvement of mass transit systems, traffic flow improvement regulations, regulations on parking lots, road and gasoline taxes, car-use permissions and incentives for voluntary approaches are mostly based on past trial-and-error experience, and include many uncertainties when trying to develop a viable transportation plan.

The clean air implementation plan should always contain an enforcement plan which indicates how the control measures can be enforced. This implies also a resource commitment which, according to a polluter pays principle, will state what the polluter has to implement and how the government will help the polluter in fulfilling the commitment.

Projections for the Future

In the sense of a precautionary plan, the clean air implementation plan should also include estimates of the trends in population, traffic, industries and fuel consumption in order to assess responses to future problems. This will avoid future stresses by enforcing measures well in advance of imagined problems.

Conclusions

In theory plans and proposals are made. Seminars and conferences are organised and conducted to create a general awareness among the public. But nothing much could have been achieved so far. So the first necessity that is needed for working out of any plan or progress for implementation is enlightening the mindset of each and every man, about what he or she can do in his own environment. Small changes can bring big results in the long-run.

4

How does Air Pollution Spread and How can we Handle this

Dr. R.N. Misra*
V.V.V. Satya Vathi**

Introduction

The dispersion of air pollutants mainly depends on physical processes in air; those of wind and weather. How far air pollutants are transported mainly depends upon particle size of the compounds and at which height the pollution was emitted into the air. Fumes that are emitted into air through high smoke stags will mix with air so that local concentrations are not very high. However, wind will transport compounds and the pollution will become very disperse. Rain can remove pollutants from air. This causes precipitation and consequentially soil and water pollution.

For environmental agencies it is very important to determine exactly how an air pollutant spreads. Air is not a very complex medium. This enables us to predict the dispersion of air pollutants with computer models. In a computer model dispersion is calculated by means of different parameters, such as wind speed, wind direction, temperature, air humidity and cloudiness. These predictions are of great significance when we are dealing with toxic clouds or radioactive radiation, because these are a danger to human health and because inhabitants of polluted areas need to be warned.

* Visiting Professor, Government College (A), Rajahmundry, E.G. Distt., A.P.

** Dept. of Commerce, Government College (A), Rajahmundry, E.G. Distt., A.P.

Any Decrease in Air Pollution leads to Longer Lives, Study Finds

"Despite the fact that the U.S. population as a whole is exposed to much lower levels of air pollution than 30 years ago - because of great strides made to reduce people's exposure - it appears that further reductions in air pollution levels would continue to benefit public health," lead author Andrew Correia said.

Numerous studies have shown that improved air quality leads to lower rates of various health problems and increases life expectancy. But because many of these studies were conducted between 1980 and 2000, when U.S. air pollution levels were steadily declining, some researchers have questioned whether the much smaller decreases that have occurred in this century would still have a health benefit.

The new study focused on levels of fine particulate matter, known as PM2.5 (indicating that the particles have diameters of 2.5 micrometers or less). It is well-established that both acute and chronic exposure to PM2.5 is associated with a higher risk of cardiovascular and lung disease and death.

The researchers examined PM2.5 levels and life expectancy statistics in 545 counties across the United States between the years 2000 and 2007. In doing so, they expanded on a 2009 *New England Journal of Medicine* study that had found an association between increased life expectancy and reduced air pollution in 211 urban counties. In addition to examining more counties, the new study made use of more recent data and was able to examine both urban and rural areas.

Pollution Control Prolongs Life

Even after controlling for other risk factors such as smoking prevalence, socio-economic status and other demographic characteristics, the researchers found that every reduction of 10 micrograms per cubic meter of PM2.5 concentration increased the average life expectancy in a county by 0.35 years.

Decreases in air pollution appeared to improve the health of women more than men.

The connection between improved air quality and life expectancy was stronger in more urban and densely populated regions. Although the reasons for this were not clear, the researchers suggested that perhaps particulate matter in urban areas has a different composition than that in rural areas.

The study strongly demonstrates that continuing to decrease levels of air pollution has a measurable and significant benefit for human health and life span.

"Since the 1970s, enactment of increasingly stringent air quality controls has led to improvements in ambient air quality in the United States at costs that the U.S. *Environmental Protection Agency* has estimated as high as $25 billion per year," senior author Francesca Dominici said. However, the extent to which more recent regulatory actions have benefited public health [had remained] in question.

What are the Main Environmental Effects of Air Pollution?

Here, we will sum up and briefly explain the main environmental effects of air pollution:

Acid Deposition

Acid deposition is not merely characterized as acid rain; it can also be snow and fog or gas and dust. Acid deposition mainly forms during fossil fuel combustion. When emissions of sulphur dioxide and nitrogen oxides come in contact with water, they will become sulphuric acid and nitric acid.

When acidifying agents, such as sulphur dioxide, nitrogen oxides and ammonia, end up in plants, surface water and soils, this has a number of consequences:

- Availability of nutrients and metal spores is likely to decrease.
- When acidity is high more metals will dissolve in water. This can cause surface water to become polluted, which has serious health effects on aquatic plants and animals. For example, high aluminum (Al) concentra-

tions can complicate nutrients uptake by plants. This makes aluminum one of the prior causes of forest decay. Mercury can be dispersed by transport through surface water, causing it to accumulate in fish. Mercury can bio magnify up the food chain, to be taken up by humans eventually.

- Buildings and monuments may be damaged through erosion. Sulphur dioxide breaks down limestone by reacting with calcium carbonate, causing limestone to absorb water during rainfall. Limestone will than fragment.

Eutrophication

Eutrophication is caused by an increase in plant nutrients in water. The higher availability of nutrients causes certain water plants, such as algae and duckweed, to grow so extensively. This blocks sunlight supplies to water. The plants also use all available oxygen supplies, which will not be renewed because heterotrophic plants and bacteria need light to perform photosynthesis. Eutrophication causes ecosystem disruption. Nitrogen pollutants such as nitrogen oxides and ammonia contribute to this problem.

Smog

Smog is a combination of the words smoke and fog. We can distinguish two separate types of smog, summer smog and winter smog.

Photochemical smog, or summer smog, mainly consists of ozone. It is a brown, oxidising fog. The causes of photochemical smog are nitrogen oxides and VOC, which stem from traffic and industries. Ozone is formed according to the following chemical reactions:

$$NO_2 + uv \rightarrow NO + O$$

$$O + O_2 \rightarrow O_3$$

The reverse reaction is:

$$NO + O_3 \rightarrow NO_2 + O_2$$

The best circumstances for the creation of high ozone concentrations are summer temperatures, direct sunlight and standing air layer, which enable dilution of contaminants. Humans cannot adapt to smog. Health effects of smog greatly depend upon the concentrations of ozone and other photochemical oxidants. These contaminants cause eye and respiratory irritations. Plants are extremely vulnerable to ozone. Even in low concentrations it can cause serious damage.

Winter smog is also referred to as acid smog; it mainly consists of foggy elements. Winter smog is found in areas where vertical dispersion of air pollutants is not possible. Usually temperatures decrease during the day in high air layers. Heated air layers near the earths' surface rise, causing the air pollutants to be dispersed vertically, and to be diluted. In winter ground temperatures are sometimes lower than those of the upper atmospheric layers, causing the air to stay near the ground, so that pollutants will not spread. This causes winter smog.

Winter smog can form when temperatures are low and sulphur dioxide concentrations increase consequential to central heater emissions from houses. The cold outside air will cause moist to condensate into fog. Aerosols in air play a part in this process, because they serve as condensation cores for water vapour. Humidity aids the transfer of sulphur dioxide to sulphuric acid, causing the smog to be acid. Acid smog causes breathing problems and eye irritations.

Ozone Loss

Ozone is created everywhere in the atmosphere through chemical reactions under the influence of UV-light. Ozone is decomposed under the influence of visible light and UV-A light. During ozone decomposition an oxygen-poor molecule is released, which aids the breakdown of ozone. There are a number of compounds that catalyse ozone decomposition. Examples are hydroxide (OH), nitrogen oxides, chlorine (Cl) and bromine (Br). Chlorine mainly aids the decomposition of ozone when it is a part of CFC-bonds (Chloro-Fluor-Carbohydrates). These compounds are not lost during the chemical reaction, causing them to decompose ozone multiple times. The decomposition and production of ozone is a natural process. However, human activities have caused large concentrations of ozone-decomposing chemicals to enter the atmosphere, causing the natural balance to be disrupted.

Ozone is very important for all life on earth, because it absorbs harmful UV-B radiation from the sun. The highest concentrations of ozone are located in the atmospheric layer between twenty and forty kilometres above the earth. When the ozone concentrations in this layer decrease, UV-B radiation may reach the earth. This radiation damages DNA and causes skin cancer. The radiation can also damage the human immune system, causing humans to become more susceptible to infections. UV-B radiation also causes cataract and near-sightedness.

5

Practices to Reduce Air Pollution

Prof. G. Chandrayya*

We make choices everyday that can help to reduce air pollution. Below are a few ideas that you can take to help clean our air:

At Home

- Conserve energy - turn off appliances and lights when you leave the room.
- Recycle paper, plastic, glass bottles, cardboard, and aluminum cans. (This conserves energy and reduces production emissions.)
- Keep woodstoves and fireplaces well maintained. You should also consider placing old wood stoves with EPA-certified models.
- Plant deciduous trees in locations around your home to provide shade in the summer, but to allow light in the winter.
- Buy green electricity-produced by low or even zero-pollution facilities.
- Connect your outdoor lights to a timer or use solar lighting.
- Wash clothes with warm or cold water instead of hot.
- Lower the thermostat on your water heater to 120F.

* Dept. of Commerce, Government College (A), Rajahmundry, A.P.

- Use low-VOC or water-based paints, stains, finishes, and paint strippers.
- Test your home for radon-a dangerous, radioactive gas that is odourless and tasteless. If the test shows elevated levels of radon, the problem can be fixed cost effectively.
- Choose not to smoke in your home, especially if you have children. If you or your visitors must smoke, then smoke outside.

Buy Smart

- Buy ENERGY STAR products, including energy efficient lighting and appliances. They are environmentally friendly products. For more information.
  - Choose efficient, low-polluting models of vehicles.
  - Choose products that have less packaging and are reusable.
  - Shop with a canvas bag instead of using paper and plastic bags.
  - Buy rechargeable batteries for devices used frequently.

Drive Wise

Plan your trips. Save gasoline and reduce air pollution.

- Keep tires properly inflated and aligned.
- In the summer time, fill gas tank during cooler evening hours to cut down on evaporation. Avoid spilling gas and don't "top off the tank. Replace gas tank cap tightly.
- Avoid waiting in long drive-thru lines, for example, at fast-food restaurants or banks. Park your car and go in.
- When possible, use public transportation, walk, or ride a bike.
- Get regular engine tune ups and car maintenance checks (especially for the spark plugs).

- Use an energy-conserving (EC) grade motor oil.
- Ask your employer to consider flexible work schedules or telecommuting.
- Report smoking vehicles to your local air agency.
- Join a carpool or vanpool to get to work.

For Your Health

- Check daily air quality forecasts, which tell how clean or polluted your air is, and the associated health concerns.
- Remove indoor asthma triggers from your home and avoid outdoor triggers in order to effectively control your asthma, to learn more about asthma triggers and ways to avoid them.
- Minimize your sun exposure. Wear sun block and UV protection sunglasses. To find out about current forecasts of UV where you live, pollution prevention, monitoring and solution.

Solution efforts on pollution is always a big problem. This is why prevention. Interventions are always a better way of controlling air pollution. These prevention methods can either come from government (laws) or by individual actions. In many big cities, monitoring equipment have been installed at many points in the city. Authorities read them regularly to check the quality of air. Let's see more below:

- **Government (or community) level prevention:** Governments throughout the world have already taken action against air pollution by introducing green energy. Some governments are investing in wind energy and solar energy, as well as other renewable energy, to minimize burning of fossil fuels, which cause heavy air pollution.
- Governments are also forcing companies to be more responsible with their manufacturing activities, so that even though they still cause pollution, they are a lot controlled.

- Companies are also building more energy efficient cars, which pollute less than before.
- **Individual Level Prevention:** Encourage your family to use the bus, train or bike when commuting. If we all do this, there will be less cars on road and less fumes.
- Use energy (light, water, boiler, kettle and fire woods) wisely. This is because lots of fossil fuels are burned to generate electricity, and so if we can cut down the use, we will also cut down the amount of pollution we create.
- **Recycle and re-use things:** This will minimize the dependence of producing new things. Remember manufacturing industries create a lot of pollution, so if we can re-use things like shopping plastic bags, clothing, paper and bottles, it can help.

Basic Air Pollution Facts

Below are some random facts and information on environmental pollution:

- Air pollutants (dangerous things that make the air unclean) come in the form of gases or particles.
- In March 2011, a very powerful earthquake in the sea (tsunami) hit the Japan coast. The sea level rose and water came into the land, damaging 4 of the 6 reactors in the Fukushima Daiichi Nuclear Power Plant.
- World Health Organisation (WHO) experts confirm that there is slight increased risk of some cancer types for some people who were exposed to the radiation. These included people living in that area and some workers at the plant. Below is a piece of the information given on BBC website:

  "The biggest lifetime risks were seen in those exposed as infants, compared with children or adults.
- For girls exposed to radiation from the accident as infants, the report found a 4 per cent increase above

the lifetime expected risk of solid tumours and a 6 per cent increase above that expected for breast cancer.

Boys exposed as infants are expected to have a 7 per cent increased risk of leukaemia above that expected in the normal population.

The biggest risk was seen in thyroid cancer, which for infant girls could be up to 70 per cent higher than expected over their lifetime."

- It is estimated that you breathe 20,000 liters of air each day. This means the more polluted the air is, the more we breathe into our lungs dangerous chemicals.
- Air can be polluted both indoors and outdoors. Tobacco and other kinds of smoking are examples of indoor air pollution.
- Sick Building Syndrome is a health condition related to pesticides, insecticides and chemicals we use at home and offices.
- In the great "Smog Disaster" in London in 1952, four thousand people died in a few days due to the high concentrations of pollution.
- Air pollution affects kids more than adults because, for their body size, kids breathe more air and spend more time playing outside.
- More hazardous pollutants are discharged into the air each year than are released to surface water, ground water, and land, combined.
- Motor vehicles produce more air pollution than any other single human activity. One full commuter bus can mean 40 less cars going through your neighbourhood.
- In America, vehicle exhaust contributes roughly 60 per cent of all carbon monoxide emissions nationwide, and up to 95 per cent in cities.

Indoor Air Pollution and Health

- Around 3 billion people cook and heat their homes using open fires and leaky stoves burning biomass (wood, animal dung and crop waste) and coal.

- Nearly 2 million people die prematurely from illness attributable to indoor air pollution from household solid fuel use.
- Nearly 50 per cent of pneumonia deaths among children under five are due to particulate matter inhaled from indoor air pollution.
- More than one million people a year die from chronic obstructive respiratory disease (COPD) that develop due to exposure to such indoor air pollution.
- Both women and men exposed to heavy indoor smoke are 2-3 times more likely to develop COPD.

Air pollution threatens the health of humans and other living beings in our planet. It creates smog and acid rain, causes cancer and respiratory diseases, reduces the ozone layer atmosphere and contributes to global warming.

Causes of Air Pollution

- Air pollution is caused when air in the atmosphere is filled with particulate matter.
- The largest source of air pollution in cities is from vehicle exhaust fumes.
- Carbon monoxide is the largest air pollutant in the United States, and it's number one source is from vehicle exhausts.
- Carbon monoxide is a poisonous, odourless, colourless gas that is formed when burning fossil fuels such as coal, petroleum and natural gas.
- Filters that are not changed regularly in your air conditioning units will accumulate dirt and cause the spread of pollutants in the air you breathe inside your home.
- Chemicals and toxic pollutants such as sulfur dioxide, nitrogen oxides and carbon dioxide react with water molecules in the atmosphere to produce acid rain. These pollutants come from factories, automobiles and any industrial or manufacturing plants.

- Another source of air pollution is from dust and dirt that goes airborne due to every day labour in the agricultural and construction industry. Dust is lifted from tractors working on fields, and from land clearing and general demolition in the construction industry.
- Using household chemicals without adequate ventilation is a major source of indoor air pollution.
- Volcanoes, dust storms, and forest fires are causes of natural air pollution.

Effects of Air Pollution

- Air pollution causes irritation in the throat, nose, lungs and eyes. It causes breathing problems and aggravates existing health conditions such as emphysema and asthma.
- Contaminated air reduces the body's defenses and decreases the body's capacity to fight other infections in the respiratory system.
- Frequent exposure to polluted air increases the risk of cardiovascular disease. Breathing air that is filled with fine particulate matter can induce hardening of the arteries, triggering cardiac arrhythmia or even a heart attack.
- People who exercise outdoors are susceptible to the adverse effects of air pollution because it involves deeper and faster breathing.
- Acid rain contains hydrogen ions, which can damage trees, crops, harm marine animals and induce corrosion in metals.
- Smog causes harmful health effects in humans and animals. Studies have shown signs of black lung disease in dolphins of due to high concentrations of carbon particles in the air.
- People afflicted with heart disease, children and older people are more sensitive to air pollution.

Air Pollution – Facts and Statistics

- Air pollution affects kids more than adults due to higher concentrations of polluted air in their systems per body size.
- India is the country with the worst air quality in the world.
- The European Union would save 161 billion Euros a year if deaths caused by air pollution were diminished.
- In large cities, over 80 per cent of fatal pollutants that cause lung damage come from cars, buses, motorcycles and other vehicles on the road.
- According to the World Health Organization, there are as many deaths (1.3 million per year) in the world due to air pollution as there are deaths due to car accidents.
- The average adult breathes 3,000 gallons of air every day.
- Each weekend, more than 800 million gallons of gas per year are used in lawn mowers in the United States, producing up to 5 per cent of total air pollution.
- Vehicle exhaust contributes 60 per cent of all carbon monoxide emissions in the United States and can go to over 90 per cent for large cities.
- The Great Smog of London in 1952 was one of the worst air pollution events in history with over 8,000 deaths.
- The largest cause of air pollution in Europe is road transportation with over 5,000 people dying each year from lung cancer and heart attacks caused by vehicle exhaust fumes.

Here are few essential ways that will help to prevent air, water and land pollution.

Practical Ways for Prevention Pollution

Prevention of air pollution

(*i*) Using smokeless sources of energy like smokeless stoves, which use biogas, solar energy, etc.

(*ii*) Using devices for filtering smoke in chimneys of factories and powerhouses.

(*iii*) Planting more trees.

(*iv*) Locating industries away from residential areas.

(*v*) Strictly checking pollution levels in automobiles' exhaust emission.

Prevention of water pollution

Water pollution is caused by dumping of domestic sewage, industrial wastes and detergents into water bodies and flow of harmful chemicals like insecticides, herbicides in water.

(*i*) Adequate sewage and industrial waste treatment in sewage treatment plants before dumping them into river bodies.

(*ii*) Recycling-various products should be recycled instead of dumping them into rivers, *e.g.*, biogas can be made from city waste.

Prevention of land pollution

Land pollution is caused by solid wastes like city wastes, crop residues, and industrial wastes like fly ash, chemicals like fertilizers and pesticides and polythene bags.

(*i*) Proper solid waste disposal like sanitary landfill.

(*ii*) Using limited amounts of fertilizers and pesticides.

(*iii*) Avoiding polythene bags.

It is high time we realized that we need the environment for our own survival and for the survival of other life forms. Hence, we must learn to respect nature and try not to disrupt its ecological balance.

In order to do so it is necessary to first have a good understanding of all the three elements of the physical environment. In the next few chapters, we shall study about land, air and water.

How the Clean Air Act is Working?

There are several ways you can tell how well the Clean Air Act is working. Over time, the Clean Air Act will continue to reduce air pollution, but it will take time for some of the Act's provisions to have their full impact.

In general, when EPA or state, local, and tribal governments require sources of pollution to adopt control measures, you will see results right away. For instance, when large industrial facilities are required to install pollution control equipment, releases of pollutants should drop when the equipment is installed. On the other hand, in the case of cars and trucks, it may take several years for old vehicles to be retired from the road before the full effects of cleaning up cars and trucks will be seen.

You can also check on how individual facilities are meeting their clean-up requirements. Air pollutant releases at individual facilities such as power plants are set out in the facility's permit, which you can review. This document provides information on state, local, or tribal air pollution control agencies that can give you more information on how to get access to permits.

Monitoring air quality is the best way to tell if the air is getting cleaner, because the monitors accurately report how much of a pollutant is in the air. You can request EPA, state, local, or tribal monitoring reports that show changes over time. It is updated frequently, so you can get recent information on what's happening to the air in your community.

The "Air Quality Index" (AQI) is a "public-friendly" way of using actual monitoring data to help us assess how clean our air is. Americans are familiar with many radio, TV, and newspaper weather forecasters talking about the AQI- telling you that the air is so polluted that a "Code Orange" or "Code Red" air quality condition is in effect. The AQI tracks pollution for your local area. The colour codes, which range from green to purple, correspond to specific pollution levels. As clean-up programs are implemented for the air pollutants tracked by the AQI, we hope to see a reduction in the number of Code Orange and Code Red air quality days.

Reducing Toxic Air Pollutants

Toxic air pollutants, or air toxics, are known to cause or are suspected of causing cancer, birth defects, reproduction problems, and other serious illnesses. Exposure to certain levels of some toxic air pollutants can cause difficulty in breathing, nausea or other illnesses. Exposure to certain toxic pollutants can even cause death.

Some toxic air pollutants are of concern because they degrade slowly or not at all, as in the case of metals such as mercury or lead. These persistent air toxics can remain in the environment for a long time and can be transported great distances. Toxic air pollutants, like mercury or polychlorinated biphenyls, deposited onto soil or into lakes and streams persist and bioaccumulate in the environment. They can affect living systems and food chains, and eventually affect people when they eat contaminated food. This can be particularly important for American Indians or other communities where cultural practices or subsistence life styles are prevalent.

The majority of air toxics come from manmade sources, such as factory smokestack emissions and motor vehicle exhaust.

Gasoline also contains air toxics. When you put fuel in your car, gases escape and form a vapor. You can smell these vapors when you refuel your vehicle.

When cars and trucks burn gasoline, toxic air pollutants are emitted from the tailpipe. Those air toxics are combustion products - chemicals that are produced when gasoline is burned. EPA is working with industries to develop cleaner-burning fuels and more efficient engines, and is taking steps to make sure that pollution control devices installed in motor vehicles work properly. EPA has issued requirements that are leading to cleaner-burning diesel engines, reducing releases of particle pollution and air toxics.

Air toxics are also released from industrial sources, such as chemical factories, refineries, and incinerators, and even from small industrial and commercial sources, such as dry cleaners and printing shops. Under the 1990 Clean Air Act, EPA has regulated both large and small sources of air toxics, but has mainly focused efforts on larger sources.

Before the 1990 Clean Air Act Amendments, EPA regulated air toxics one chemical at a time. This approach did not work well. Between 1970 and 1990, EPA established regulations for only seven pollutants. The 1990 Clean Air Act Amendments took a completely different approach to reducing toxic air pollutants. The Amendments required EPA to identify categories of industrial sources for 187 listed toxic air pollutants and to take steps to reduce pollution by requiring sources to install controls or change production processes. It makes good sense to regulate by categories of industries rather than one pollutant at a time, since many individual sources release more than one toxic chemical. Developing controls and process changes for industrial source categories can result in major reductions in releases of multiple pollutants at one time.

EPA has published regulations covering a wide range of industrial categories, including chemical plants, incinerators, dry cleaners, and manufacturers of wood furniture. Harmful air toxics from large industrial sources, such as chemical plants, petroleum refineries, and paper mills, have been reduced by nearly 70 percent. These regulations mostly apply to large, so-called "major" sources and also to some smaller sources known as "area" sources. In most cases, EPA does not prescribe a specific control technology, but sets a performance level based on a technology or other practices already used by the better-controlled and lower emitting sources in an industry. EPA works to develop regulations that give companies as much flexibility as possible in deciding how they reduce their toxic air emissions-as long as the companies meet the levels required in the regulations.

The 1990 Clean Air Act requires EPA to first set regulations using a technology-based or performance-based approach to reduce toxic emissions from industrial sources. After EPA sets the technology-based regulations, the Act requires EPA to evaluate any remaining ("residual") risks, and decide whether it is necessary to control the source further. That assessment of remaining risk was initiated in the year 2000 for some of the industries covered by the technology-based standards.

Chemical Emergencies

The 1984 chemical disaster that resulted in thousands of deaths in Bhopal, India, inspired sections of the 1990 Clean Air Act that require factories and other businesses to develop plans to prevent accidental releases of highly toxic chemicals.

The 1990 Act also established the Chemical Safety Board, an independent agency that investigates and reports on accidental releases of toxic chemicals from industrial facilities. The Board operates much like the National Transportation Safety Board, the agency that investigates airplane and train crashes. The Chemical Safety Board assembles the information necessary to determine how and why an accident involving toxic chemicals happened. The goal is to apply understanding of accidents to prevent other accidents involving toxic chemicals.

Air Toxics and Risk

The Clean Air Act requires a number of studies to help EPA better characterize risks to human health and the environment from air toxics. Those studies provide information for rule making and support national and local efforts to address risks through pollution prevention and other voluntary programmes. Among these risk reduction initiatives are:

- The Integrated Urban Air Toxics Strategy includes local and community-based initiatives to reduce local toxic air emissions. The primary goal of the strategy is to reduce public health risks from both indoor and outdoor sources of toxic air pollutants.

- The Great Waters Programme incorporates activities to investigate and reduce the deposition of toxic air pollutants to the "Great Waters," which include the Chesapeake Bay, Lake Champlain, the Great Lakes, National Estuary Programme areas, and National Estuarine Research Reserves.
- Initiatives targeting emission reductions of persistent bioaccumulative toxics (PBTs) like mercury, DDT (a pesticide banned in the United States), and dioxins.

Why Should You Be Concerned About Air Pollution?

You could go days without food and hours without water, but you would last only a few minutes without air. On average, each of us breathes over 3,000 gallons of air each day. You must have air to live. However, did you know that breathing polluted air can make you sick?

Air pollution can damage trees, crops, other plants, lakes, and animals. In addition to damaging the natural environment, air pollution also damages buildings, monuments, and statues. It not only reduces how far you can see in national parks and cities, it even interferes with aviation.

In 1970, Congress created the Environmental Protection Agency (EPA) and passed the Clean Air Act, giving the federal government authority to clean up air pollution in this country. Since then, EPA and states, tribes, local governments, industry, and environmental groups have worked to establish a variety of programs to reduce air pollution levels across America.

The Clean Air Act has helped change the way many of us work or do business. In some cases, it has even changed the way we live. This guide provides a brief introduction to the programs, philosophies, and policies in the Clean Air Act.

Air Pollution and Your Health

Breathing polluted air can make your eyes and nose burn. It can irritate your throat and make breathing difficult. In fact, pollutants like tiny airborne particles and groundlevel ozone can trigger respiratory problems, especially for people with asthma. Today, nearly 30 million adults and children in the United States have been diagnosed with asthma. Asthma sufferers can be severely affected by air pollution. Air pollution can also aggravate health problems for the elderly and others with heart or respiratory diseases.

Some toxic chemicals released in the air such as benzene or vinyl chloride are highly toxic and can cause cancer, birth defects, long-term injury to the lungs, as well as brain and nerve damage. And in some cases, breathing these chemicals can even cause death.

Other pollutants make their way up into the upper atmosphere, causing a thinning of the protective ozone layer. This has led to changes in the environment and dramatic increases in skin cancers and cataracts (eye damage).

Air Pollution and the Environment

Air pollution isn't just a threat to our health, it also damages our environment. Toxic air pollutants and the chemicals that form acid rain and ground-level ozone can damage trees, crops, wildlife, lakes and other bodies of water. Those pollutants can also harm fish and other aquatic life.

Air Pollution and the Economy

The health, environmental, and economic impacts of air pollution are significant. Each day, air pollution causes thousands of illnesses leading to lost days at work and school. Air pollution also reduces agricultural crop and commercial forest yields by billions of dollars each year.

6

Air Pollution

Dr. Brajamohan Sasmal*

Introduction

The God has created the universe along with the living beings (Human beings, animals, birds, insects etc.), the nature (trees, plants, jungles, landscapes, rocks, mountains, streams, rivers, seas etc.), the atmosphere and the vast sky filled with ether.

Air is a part of the atmosphere which is present above the earth's surface. Actually air is a mechanical mixture of solid particles (dust and smoke), moisture, naturally occurring chemical gases like Nitrogen (73%) , Oxygen (5-7%) and traces of rare gases. Air is highly essential for the survival of all living beings on the earth as all living beings inhale the atmospheric air during respiration. The loss of oxygen gas from the atmosphere is being usually compensated by the oxygen gas supplied from the trees and plants present in the nature. In fact, all living beings inhale oxygen gas and exhale carbon dioxide gas during their respiration. On the other hand, the plants and trees consume carbon dioxide gas from the atmosphere and prepare their carbohydrate food in presence of sunlight, water and chlorophyll present in the leaves and stems of the trees and plants. Thus, oxygen gas is produced from this process (photosynthesis) occurring in the nature and gets stored in the atmosphere and next moment it is used for the respiration of living beings.

---

* Retd. Professor, Sheragada Bunglow, Convent School Road, Brahmapur-760001.

Air Pollution

Generally in non-industrial and rural areas at normal temperature and pressure the air present in the atmosphere may be called as pure air. But, in industrial and urban areas the air present in atmosphere is called as impure air or polluted air due to the presence of chemical gases (carbon monoxide, carbon dioxide, sulphur dioxide, nitrogen oxide, hydrogen sulphide etc.), dust particles, smokes and the liquid droplets which are known as pollutants. The air pollutant is a substance when added to air causes adverse effects on the health of human beings, animals, birds, insects, aquatic animals and eco-systems. Pollutants may be poisonous solid particles, liquid droplets or gases. A pollutant may have a natural origin or manmade. Therefore pollutants as classified as primary and secondary. Primary pollutants are generally produced by the natural processes such as volcanic eruptions and burning of organic fuels like coals, wood, dried crop wastes and cow dungs. Other examples of primary air pollutants are carbon monoxide, carbon dioxide gases produced from the motor vehicle exhausts or sulphur dioxide gas released from factory chimneys. The secondary pollutants are not emitted directly but are formed in the atmospheric air by the chemical interactions of primary pollutants with the chemical gases already present in the atmospheric air. Any type of pollutant present in pure air causes pollution and becomes a threat to human health, animal health, aquatic animal health and earth's eco-system.

As "the prevention is better than cure", men and government authorities must be careful now onwards to prevent the air pollution, otherwise the survival of the living beings will be impossible on this earth.

Sources

1. Poisonous gases emitted by natural processes such as volcanic eruptions, burning of organic fuels like wood, dried crop wastes, cow dungs and coal contain mostly carbon dioxide, sulphur dioxide, smoke and particles of heavy metals causing high pollution of air.

2. Smoke produced from the chimney of power plants, factories and furnaces contain sulphur dioxide, carbon monoxide, nitrogen dioxide, hydrogen sulphide, the particles of zinc, lead, molybdenum metals, which pollutes atmospheric air.
3. The gaseous exhausts from motor vehicles in urban areas, marine vessels and aircrafts mostly contain carbon monoxide and carbon dioxide, which cause pollution in atmosphere air.
4. Wildfires of forest five cause pollution in atmospheric air by production of smokes, carbon dioxide gas and carbon monoxide gas.
5. Chemical fumes from paints, hair spray, varnishes and aerosol sprays cause air pollution.
6. Garbage and waste products of urban areas when dumped for a longer period in a bigger pit or vessel produce methane gas which is highly inflammable and form poisonous mixture of gases with air. It also reduces oxygen gas content from atmospheric air and causes asphyxia or suffocation.
7. Military nuclear weapons, use of tear gases use of germ warfare and launching of rockets highly pollute the atmospheric air.
8. In urban areas, generators, refrigerators, air conditioners produce most dangerous gases like fluorine gas and chlorofluorocarbon gas and polluting air to greater extent.
9. For urbanisation and installation of factories, deforestation or destruction of jungles or forests are undertaken by cutting off the huge number of bigger and smaller trees. This causes ecological imbalances, global warming and highly reduces the supply of oxygen to the atmospheric air.
10. In industrial areas the atmospheric air contains mostly sulphur dioxide, nitrogen dioxide gases, which are

emitted from the chimneys of the furnaces of factories. On rainy days the rain water reacts with these gases of the air and produce acids such as sulphuric acid and nitric acid which are highly corrosive and impervious to human skin aquatic animals, leaves of crops due to the acid rain effect.

Hazardous Effects

Air pollution risk is a function of the hazards of the pollutants and the exposure to pollutants. Air pollution exposure may be for an individual, for certain groups (Neighbouring families or children) or for the entire population of a city or village. The air pollution exposure includes different age and other demographic groups especially infants, children, pregnant women and other sensitive subpopulations. According to World Health Organisation (WHO), air pollution is a significant risk factor for a multiple health conditions including respiratory infections, heart disease and lung cancer. The health effects caused by air pollution may include difficulty in breathing, wheezing, coughing, asthma and aggravation of existing respiratory and cardiac conditions. These effects cause result in increased medication use, increase doctor's care or emergency room visits, more hospitalisation and premature deaths. The human health effects of poor air quality are far reaching, but principally affect the body's respiratory system and the cardiovascular system. The World Health Organisation states that about 2.4. million people die each year from causes directly attributable to indoor and outdoor air pollutions.

Prevention

According to World Health Organisation (WHO), air pollution is mainly believed to be manmade. So man can only take preventive measures to reduce air pollution and it is high time for human to think for a better future life of living beings on this earth. Some important measures for prevention of air pollution are given below:

- Reduce the use of vehicles either by resorting to public transport for daily transportation or switching over from vehicles to other means such as cycling or walking.
- If the use of vehicle is inevitable, make sure that you use it efficiently *i.e.* drive within the speed limit recommended by the manufacturer, turn the engine off on red light and make sure that you maintain your vehicle as per their instructions.
- Buying fuel efficient vehicles is yet another option that you have. Several car manufacturers are using advanced technology to roll out vehicles, which minimize emissions of smoke and gaseous pollutants.
- Implement practices such as 'carpool' wherein you take turns to use your vehicles in your neighbourhood or workplace. Simple, but effective measure when it comes to vehicle pollution.
- Though indirectly saving energy by resorting to energy saving appliances and not wasting electricity will also help in carbine air pollution lesser the energy requirements lesser will be produced and thus turn, will lessen the amount of air pollution caused by power plants or furnaces.
- Do not burn the wastes generated in your homes instead resort to other means of garbage disposal. The same rule implies when it comes to disposal of your garden wastes or home garbage. A better way out is to opt for traditional methods such as composting but putting them in a bigger pit.
- You can also resort to technology advanced air pollution control equipment systems such as use of wet scrubbers to remove acid gases present in the atmospheric air.
- Use a thermostat in your homes so that your heater or air conditioner automatically gets switched off when it is not required.

- Follow all the rules and regulations meant to stop environmental pollution and do try to spread awareness about such environmental hazards.
- To purify the polluted air my making up the deficiency of oxygen gas, every individual may be young or old must start plantations everywhere regularly and stop destruction of forest due to regular cutting off of trees.

Conclusion

Air pollution is a significant risk factor for multiple health conditions including respiratory infections, heart diseases and lung cancer. According to the WHO (World Health Organisation). The human health effects of poor air quality are really dangerous, but principally it effects the body's respiratory system and the cardiovascular system.

As "Prevention is better than cure" we must take all preventive measures for air pollution as discussed in the text. The state and the central government authorities must take strict measures against the pollution control board of such authorities who neglect their duties in preventing air pollution. These authorities must frame strict rules to accord temporary or permanent permissions to different factories and industries for installation near the township or other habitats. Forest departments must be alert enough to eradicate deforestations and regular cutting of the logs of wood by the people to get rid of the hazards of the air pollution and save the lives of human beings, animals, plants, crops, insects etc. in future days.

7
Indoor Air Pollution
(A Study)

Dr. Brajamohan Sasmal*

Introduction

The human body is the composition of five elements; *i.e.* Earth or *Prithvi;* Water or *Jal;* Fire or *Agni;* Air or *Vayu* and then Ether or *Akasha. Vayu* or Air is one of the basic ingredients of life. Perfect knowledge about air and its importance for human being, indeed very vital for the present generation. If we seriously investigate the cause of pollution, it will be clear before us that the root cause of air pollution is man. Recent researches have shown that the effect of indoor pollution is more furious compared to outdoor pollution. Report shows that indoor pollution kills millions of people every year. Indoor air pollution is the second biggest killer after high blood pressure in India. Survey says that around 1.3 million people died of indoor air pollution in 2010 whereas death because of outdoor air pollution was around 6.20 lakhs.

This era of technological the advancement is regarded as the greater gift to the mankind. But, in this happiness we forgot to notice that not only outside but; the dangerous effect of technology is found indoor today. So called intelligent man is quite unaware about the products which are really polluting the internal environment. The list starts from the regular perfume and deodorants to fresh new carpet and different cleaning products. In the wildest of their dream they never

* Retd. Professor, Sheragada Bunglow, Convent School Road, Brahmapur-760001.

thought that the insect killers which kills insect are also silently enters into our body and killing us slowly. Human beings are unknown about the chlorofluorocarbon coming out from their refrigerator and air conditioners. Smoking becomes the symbol of pride for youngsters which are another reason of killing and even polluting the environment surrounding them. Other evil products like broken Fluorescent bulbs, different new electronic devices, other plastic products, glues and adhesives, heating equipments (stoves, fire places, heaters and chimneys), paint and strippers, upholstered furniture and pressed wood products, cleaning products, air fresheners, etc. are coming under these category.

Sometime we immediately know its affect. A single exposure invites irritation of eyes, nose and throat which gradually leads to headaches, dizziness and fatigue. These effects are sometime short-lived and can be treated easily. The problem can be vanished with simply eliminating the source of pollutant from nearby areas. But, in other cases health effects can be noticed after a prolong period. These effects lead to some respiratory diseases, heart diseases, cancer, etc. So it is important to improve the Inside Air Quality (IAQ) in home and indoor areas one spends most of their time.

Literature Review

A study by WHO said that about 80 per cent of women in India are affected by indoor air pollution. The Tata Energy and Resources Institute (TERI) in a study said that 27.5 per cent of under-five infant mortality in India is because of indoor air pollution. ICMR study in Chennai shows that around 1,200 people showed an increase of 0.3 per cent to 0.6 per cent in mortality with rise in particulate matter pollution by 10 $\mu g/m^3$.

Approximately half of the world population and up to 90 per cent of rural households in developing countries still rely on unprocessed biomass fuels such as wood, dung and crop residues. This is the main source of pollution. The 1991 National Census for the first time reveled the truth about the fuel used for coking. It revealed that about 90 per cent of the rural population relied upon the biomass fuels like animal dung, crop residues and wood. A small portion used coal. Nation-wide about 78 per cent of the population relied upon the biomass fuels and 3 per cent on coal.

Objectives of the Study

- To study the factors influencing indoor air pollution.
- To know the effects of indoor air pollution.
- To find out the steps we can take to prevent indoor air pollution

Scope of the Study

- The idea of this study is to aware the ignorant man about the product responsible for indoor pollution.
- The purpose is to aware common people about the general and furious health effects of indoor air pollution.
- It recommends various ways to control the effects of indoor air pollution.

Analysis of the Study

Till today many people thinks that air pollution is caused because of automobile exhausts and industrial effluents. However, in developing countries, the problem of indoor air pollution far outweighs the ambient air pollution. The amount of exposure in terms of the number of people, exposure intensity and time spent exposed is most in the developing world (Smith, 1993); approximately 76 per cent of all global participate matter air pollution occurs indoors in the developing world.

Total global exposure to particulate matter pollution

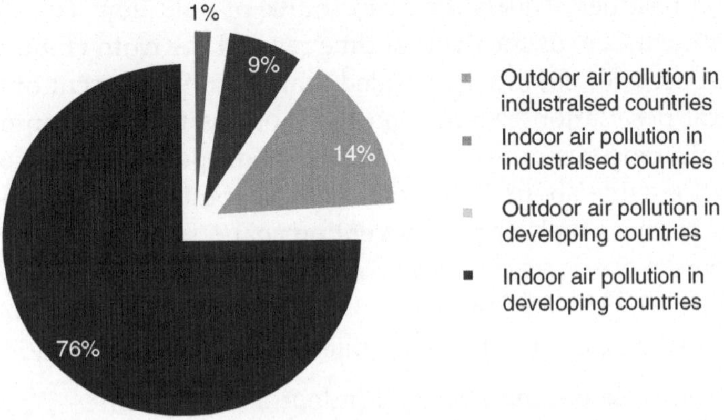

Smith K.R. Fuel combustion air pollution, exposure health the situation in developing countries. Annual review of energy environment 1B 529-566 (1993).

Sources of Pollutants

There are five primary sources of pollutants of indoor air: (1) New electronics and other plastic products, (2) Paints and strippers, (3) Cleaning products (Many house cleaners, Chemical air fresheners) (4) Combustion and (5) Tobacco smoke.

Apart from these there are many other sources like Air conditioner, refrigerator, New carpets, Shoes, creams and lotions, Candles and incense sticks, etc, Laundry detergent and fabric softeners are also coming under this category.

New Electronics and Other Plastic Products

Products made with polyvinyl chloride can emit phthalates, which have been linked to hormonal abnormalities and reproductive problems. Plastics can also release flame-retardant chemicals, such as polybrominated biphenyl ethers, which have been linked to neurobehavioral changes in animal studies.

Paints and Strippers

The ingredients in most common paint removers are organic solvents which may damage the skin, eyes, respiratory tract, nervous system, and internal organs. Special precautions must be taken in their use. Especially if there are children present who might come in contact with either the material or its vapors. Health hazards related to chemical paint removers are Respiratory System Damage, Skin Diseases, Damage to Internal Organs, Brain and Nervous System Damage, Fire Hazards.

Combustion

Indian leaders from the public health, environmental, and security sectors have been requested government to reduce household or indoor air pollution from solid fuels as a major contributor to death early in life. From the 3.5 million deaths caused due to household air pollution worldwide in 2010, many of which were in young children. India, has estimated 100,411 children died as a result of household air pollution that same year.

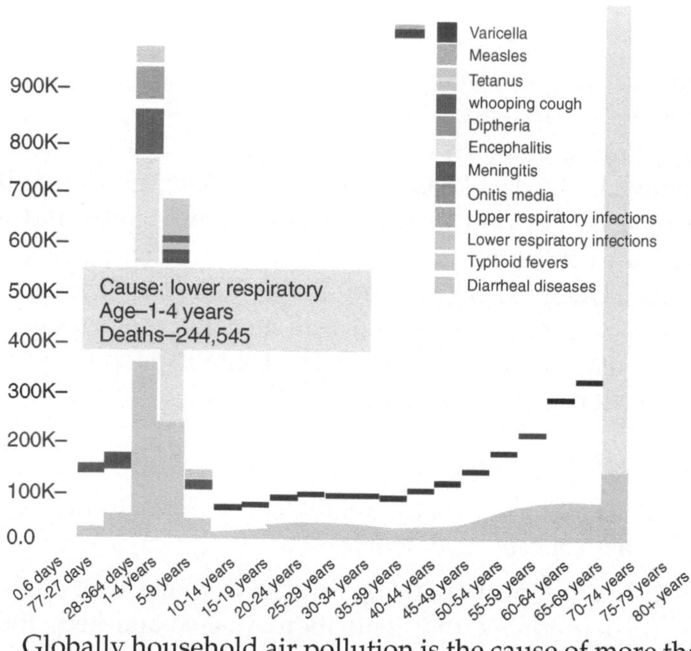

Globally household air pollution is the cause of more than 50 per cent of deaths from lower respiratory infections among the children under five. The above graphic comes from the Institute for Health Metrics and Evaluation's GBD (Global Burden of Disease) visualization tool and shows how lower respiratory infections cause many more deaths in children than in most other age groups, underscoring the potential to save a large number of lives by prioritizing interventions that reduce exposure to household air pollution.

Cleaning Products

U.S. Poison Control Centers reported nearly 10 per cent of all toxic exposures are because of cleaning products. Some cleaners are among the most toxic products found in the home. If I use the wrong ones, I have breathing issues. In 2000, there were 120,434 reported exposures involved children under six to Poison Control. They either swallowed or spilled cleaners stored or left open inside the home.

Tobacco Smoke

Tobacco smoke contains many pollutants at high concentrations. "Tobacco use kills more than five million people every year - more than HIV/AIDS, tuberculosis and malaria combined." In developed countries, smoking is responsible for over 80 per cent of cases of chronic bronchitis and for most cases of emphysema and chronic obstructive pulmonary disease. These studies showed that in India, the incidence of chronic cor pulmonale is similar in men and women despite the fact that 75 per cent of the men and only 10 per cent women are smokers.

Measures to Control

1. Install local exhaust ventilation facilities to deal with the concentrated sources.
2. Ensure proper design and construction of the air conditioning and ventilation systems and keep them in normal operation by good maintenance to provide

adequate good quality air (together with enough fresh air) at the places where it is needed.

3. Use an air exchanger or an air cleaner at special locations to improve indoor air quality.
4. Public education: make people aware of the health consequences of poor indoor air quality and the control measures needed to guarantee good indoor air quality.
5. Change in pattern of fuel use from biomass to LPG and solar cooker is highly recommended.
6. To prevent eye irritation caused by splashing, one should wear light-weight plastic splash goggles while pouring or working with paint removers.
7. Ventilation in the kitchen should be given due priority in the design of the houses. In existing houses, measures such as putting a window above the cooking stove and providing cross ventilation through the door may help in diluting the pollution load.
8. Collaboration and commitment between agencies responsible for health, energy, environment, housing and rural development.
9. Before starting a paint removal project, be sure turn off all pilot lights and remove any sources of heat, ultraviolet light, or flame in areas where vapor might drift. In addition, any source of spark or static electricity should be eliminated during use of flammable paint strippers.
10. Solvent-soaked rags should be stored in approved, self-closing oily waste cans, or immediately placed outside. Do not store inside in open wastepaper baskets. Disposal should be done in accordance with local city and fire regulations, and waste-disposal firm may be necessary for large quantities of solvent waste. Never pour solvents down the drain. Small quantities of solvents can be evaporated under a fume hood or outdoors.

11. A National Institute of Occupational Safety and Health (NIOSH)-approved respirator with organic vapor cartridges can help minimize exposure to paint remover vapors if ventilation is not adequate.
12. Gloves should be worn when using paint removers. Ordinary rubber dish washing gloves or surgical gloves will dissolve in paint remover. Neoprene/natural latex blend gloves can withstand most paint remover solvents. If you are going to use steel wool with the paint remover, use cotton gloves over the Neoprene/latex gloves to protect them from abrasion so they will last longer. To further decrease the risk of skin contact wear long pants, a long sleeve shirt and an apron.

Conclusion

Air pollution is an alarming danger, slowly which will eat the whole planet if today we will not check or reduce its causes. This paper along with other studies it is clear that the indoor air is about 76 per cent polluted today. It is not only the cause of several health diseases but also the reason of growing death. It is now the right time to come out from the mask of ignorance and spread the message in the society. Everybody should try to follow the measures to prevent indoor air pollution and make others to follow it too. In this way one day we can make our air pollution free.

REFERENCES

Chetan Chauhan, (2013) "Indoor air pollution kills a million people every year in India", Hindustan Times, New Delhi.

Eva Dong, Ramon Estrada, "Indoor air quality is it a problem at your child's school?", Sonora Environmental Research Institute, Inc.

"Indoor Air Pollution in India - a major environmental and public health concern" (2001), *ICMR bulletin*, Vol. 31, No.5, ISSN 0377-4910.

Behera, D., "Health effects of indoor air pollution due to domestic cooking fuels". *Indian J Chest Dis Allied Sci 37:* 237, 1995.

Smith, K.R. "Indoor air quality and the population transition". In: *Indoor Air Quality.* Ed. H. Kasuga. Springer Verlag, Berlin, pp. 448,1990.

Bruce, N., Perez-padilla, R. and Albalak, R. "Indoor air pollution in developing countries: A major environmental and public health challenge". *Bull World Health Organ 78:* 1078, 2000.

Smith, K., Samet, J.M., Romieu, I. and Bruce, N. "Indoor air pollution in developing countries and acute respiratory infections in children". *Thorax 55:* 518, 2000.

8

Prevention of Air Pollution

Dr. D. Tata Rao*

Introduction

Drive Less, Drive Smart About half of the air pollution conies from cars and trucks. Two important ways to reduce air pollution are to drive less—even a little less—and to drive smart. Taking fewer trips in your car or truck helps cut air pollution. And adopting smart driving habits reduces your car's emissions.

Driving less doesn't mean you have to stay home. Try combining driving with alternative modes of transportation:

1. Carpool.
2. Walk or ride a bicycle.
3. Shop by phone or mail.
4. Ride public transit.
5. Telecommunate.

Driving smart keeps pollution at a minimum.[1]

1. Accelerate gradually.
2. Use cruise control on the highway.
3. Obey the speed limit.

---

* Principal, Government Degree College Chipurapalli, Vizinagaram District, A.P.

** What do you when you are stuck in traffic and not "driving" can be very important as well. Consider turning your engine off it you will be idling for long periods of time. That's not all. When shopping for your next car...

4. Combine your errands into one trip.
5. Keep your car tuned and support the smog check program.
6. Don't top off at the gas pumps.
7. Replace your car's air filter.
8. Keep your tires properly inflated.
9. What about smoking vehicles?
10. Look for the most efficient, lowest polluting model—or even use either a non-polluting car or zero emission vehicle.

If you must drive on days with unhealthy air, drive your newest car. Newer cars generally pollute less than older models.

Choose Air-Friendly Products: Many products you use in your home, in the yard, or at the office are made with smog-forming chemicals that escape into the air. Here are a few ways to put a lid on products that pollute:

1. Select products that are water-based or have low amounts of volatile organic compounds (VOCs).
2. Use water-based paints. Look for paints labelled "zero-VOC."
3. Paint with a brush, not a sprayer.
4. Store solvents in air-tight containers.
5. Use a push or electric lawn mower.
6. Start your barbecue briquettes with an electric probe, or use a propane or natural gas barbecue.

Save Energy

Saving energy helps reduce air pollution. Whenever you burn fossil fuel, you pollute the air. Use less gasoline, natural gas, and electricity (power plants burn fossil fuels to generate electricity):

1. Turn off the lights when you leave a room.

2. Replace energy hungry incandescent lights with fluorescent lighting.
3. Check with your utility company for energy conservation tips, like purchasing energy saving appliances.
4. Use a thermostat that automatically turns off the air conditioner or heater when you don't need them.
5. Add insulation to your home.
6. Use a fan instead of air conditioning.
7. Use an EPA-approved wood burning stove or fireplace insert.
8. Heat small meals in a microwave oven.
9. Insulate your water heater.
10. Install low flow showerheads.
11. Dry your clothes on a clothesline.

Waste Not

It takes energy to make and sell the products we use. Here are ways to cut energy use, reduce air pollution, and save money.

1. Choose recycled products.
2. Choose products with recyclable packaging.
3. Reuse paper bags.
4. Recycle paper, plastics, and metals.
5. Print and photocopy on both sides of the paper.

Watch Out For The Small Stuff

When you breathe, very small particles—such as dust, soot, and acid droplets—can slip past your lung's natural defense system. These particles get stuck deep in your lungs and may cause problems—more asthma attacks, bronchitis and other lung diseases, decreased resistance to infections, and even premature death for the elderly or sick. Here are a few things you can do to reduce particulate matter pollution and protect yourself:

1. Don't use your wood stove or fireplace on days with unhealthy air.
2. Avoid using leaf blowers and other types of equipment that raise a lot of dust. Use a rake or broom instead.
3. Drive slowly on unpaved roads.
4. Drive less, particularly on days with unhealthy air.
5. Avoid vigorous physical activity on days with unhealthy air.

Know the Inside Story

Air pollution is a problem indoors and out. Most people spend at least 80 per cent of their lives indoors. Here are some ways you can reduce pollution in your home, office or school:

1. Don't smoke. Send smokers outside.
2. Products such as cleaning agents, paints, and glues often contain harmful chemicals. Use them outdoors or with plenty of ventilation indoors.
3. Use safer products, such as baking soda instead of harsher chemical cleaners.
4. Don't heat your home with a gas cooking stove.
5. Have your gas appliances and heater regularly inspected and maintained.
6. Clean frequently to remove dust and molds.

Speak Up for Clean Air

Do what you can to reduce air pollution. It will make a difference. Use your civic influence to improve regional and national air pollution standards:

1. Write to your local newspaper. Support action for healthy air.
2. Let your elected representative know you support action for clean air.

What Causes Air Pollution?

The main sources of air pollution are the industries, agriculture and traffic, as well as energy generation. During combustion processes and other production processes air pollutants are emitted. Some of these substances are not directly damaging to air quality, but will form harmful air pollutants by reactions with other substances that are present in air.

Examples of large-scale air pollutants are VOC (Volatile Organic Compounds) and small dust particles. When large concentrations of these substances are emitted this negatively affects ecosystems, materials and public health.

Emissions of nitrous oxide (N_2O) mainly stem from agriculture, because nitrogen in soils can easily be denitrified by bacteria. Nitrous oxide is emitted during the denitrification process. Additionally, the application of (artificial) fertilizers causes emissions of ammonia (NHa), nitrogen oxides (NO_X) and methane (CH_4), a greenhouse gas. The agricultural sector is known for its extensive use of pesticides. This application causes emissions of many toxic chemicals.

Industrial processes vary greatly and as a result there are many different chemical wastes. The industries are responsible for emissions of carbon monoxide, carbon dioxide, sulphur dioxide, nitrogen oxides, small dust particles, VOC, methane, ammonia and radioactive radiation.

During energy generation chemicals such as methane are released into the air as a result of oil and natural gas extraction. The combustion of coal and natural gas for electricity production causes the release of sulphur dioxide, nitrogen oxides and carbon dioxide into the air.

Traffic is held responsible for one-third of the greenhouse gas emissions. Emissions caused by traffic are mainly those of carbon dioxide, carbon monoxide, nitrogen oxides, VOC and small dust particles.

Consumers are also partly responsible for air pollution. Firstly because the products they use have caused air pollution during their production and distribution and secondly because heating of houses and offices causes chemicals release into the air. When people use paints or cosmetics VOC is released and perspiration, pet fertilizer use and cleanser use cause ammonia emissions. Last but not least, many chemicals (carbon dioxide, carbon monooxide) are emitted during smoking.

How does Air Pollution Form?

Air pollution can form in various ways. Chemicals are emitted during many different human activities. In the atmosphere these chemicals can react with other chemicals to more dangerous substances. Air pollutants often have properties that are harmful to the environment.

The weather plays an important role in the formation and disappearance of air pollution. This is mainly influenced by wind and temperatures. Air pollutants can be transported by wind, causing a pollution to spread widely. Rain can remove pollutants from air, causing soil and water pollution. Sunlight can aid the convention of air pollutants to different substances.

Chemicals can come from various sources, and are formed during different processes. Air pollution can be divided in categories according to the source it is derived from:

- Biological air pollution, such as pollens, small insects and microrganisms (bacteria, fungi, yeasts and algae).
- Physical air pollution, such as sound, smell, thermal pollution and radioactive radiation.
- Chemical air pollution, such as ozone, aerosols and ammonia.

Air pollution is caused by both human and natural sources. Human sources are traffic, agriculture or industry, as was mentioned before. Natural sources are be dust storms, volcanic eruptions and emissions from plants.

Air pollution undergoes a number of processes:

- Emission (contaminants are released into the air)

- Transport (contaminants are transported to different locations through air)
- Exchange (compounds react with other compounds in air)
- Distribution (contaminants are distributed in air)
- Immission (contaminants maintain in a certain area)
- Deposition (contaminants are deposited in a certain area, on the soil or on objects)

What Types of Air Pollution are There?

Air pollution consists of gases and/or particles. These have a distinct chemical or physical structure, or a distinct effect on human health.

The main air contaminants are:

- **Sulphur dioxide (SO_2).** This contaminant is mainly emitted during the combustion of sulphur-containing fossil fuels, such as crude oil and coal. Sulphur dioxide concentrations in air have decreased in the past two decades, mainly because we use more non-sulphur-containing fuels for the generation of energy. Sulphur dioxide is a stinging gas and as a result it can cause breathing problems with humans. In moist environments, sulphur dioxide may be transferred to sulphuric acid. This acid causes acidification and winter smog.
- **Nitrogen oxides (NO_X).** These contaminants are emitted by traffic, combustion installations, such as power plants, and the industries. Nitrogen oxides are also released from farmland in the agricultural sector. Using catalysers in car exhausts can prevent emissions of nitrogen oxides. Nitrogen oxides are gasses that react with other air pollutants when they are present in air. For example, nitrogen oxides play an important role in the formation of ozone in the lower atmosphere, and in acidification and eutrophication processes. They can deeply penetrate the lungs and damage human lung functions.

- Ammonia (NH_3). Ammonia forms during agricultural activities. Ammonia plays an important role in acidification and eutrophication.
- **VOC (Volatile Organic Compounds).** VOC can be a range of different contaminants, such as carbohydrates, organic compounds and solvents. These compounds usually derive from petrol and gasoline reservoirs, industrial processes and fuel combustion, paint and cleanser use, or agricultural activities. VOC play an important role in ozone shaping in the lower atmospheric layer, the main cause of smog. VOC can cause various health effects, depending on the kind of compounds that are present and their concentrations. Effects can vary from smell nuisance to decreases in lung capacity, and even cancer.
- **Methane (CH_4).** The main source of methane pollution is agriculture. But smaller amounts of methane can also be released during waste combustion and natural gas extraction. Methane is a greenhouse gas that contributes to the greenhouse effect and ozone loss.
- **Carbon monoxide (CO).** This gas consists during incomplete combustion of fuels. When we let a car engine run in a closed room, carbon monoxide concentrations in the air will rise extensively. Carbon monoxide contributes to the greenhouse effect, smog and acidification. The gas can bind to haemoglobin in blood, preventing oxygen transport through the body. This results in oxygen depletion of the heart, brains and blood vessels, eventually causing death.
- **Dust particles.** Dust particles form a complex of organic compounds and minerals. These can derive from natural sources, such as volcanoes, or human activities, such as industrial combustion processes or traffic. Particles are categorised according to particle size. The smallest particles have the ability to transport toxic compounds into the respiratory tract. Some of these compounds

are carcinogenic. The upper respiratory tract stops the larger dust particles. When they are released into the environment, dust particles can cause acidification and winter smog.

- **Ozone (O_3).** Ozone is created through photochemical transfer of oxygen. This process takes place under the influence of ultra violet sunlight (UV), aided by pollutants in the outside air. Ozone causes smog and contributes to acidification and climate change. Ozone is an aggressive gas. Which can easily penetrate the respiratory tract, deeply. When humans are exposed to ozone, the consequences may be irritation of the eyes and the respiratory tract.
- **Radioactive radiation.** Radioactive radiation and radioactive particles are naturally present in the environment. During power plant incidents or treatments of nuclear waste from a war where nuclear weapons are used, radioactive radiation can enter the air on account of humans. When humans are exposed to high levels of radioactive radiation, the chances of serious health effects are very high. Radioactive radiation can cause DNA alteration and cancer.

REFERENCES

Andersen, Z. J., Kristiansen, L. C., Andersen, K. K., Olsen, T. S., Hvidberg, M., Jensen, S. S., Raaschou-Nielsen, O. (2011). Stroke and Long-Term Exposure to Outdoor Air Pollution From Nitrogen Dioxide: A Cohort Study. Stroke; a journal of cerebral circulation.

Brook, R. D.; Rajagopalan, S; Pope, CA III; Brook, JR; Bhatnagar, A (2010). "Particulate matter air pollution and cardiovascular disease: An update to the scientific statement from the American Heart Association". *Circulation* **121:** 2331-2378.

Christopher H. Goss, Stacey A. Newsom, Jon athan S. Schildcrout, Lianne Sheppard and Joel D. Kaufrnan (2004). "Effect of Ambient Air Pollution on Pulmonary Exacerbations and Lung Function in Cystic Fibrosis". *American Journal of Respiratory and Critical Care Medicine* **169** (7): 816-821.

Louwies, T; Int Panis, L; Kicinski, M; De Boever, P; Nawrot, Tim S (2013). "Retinal Microvascular Responses to Short-Term Changes in Particulate Air Pollution in Healthy Adults". *Environmental Health Perspectives.*

Miller K. A., Siscovick D. S., Sheppard L., Shepherd K., Sullivan J. H., Anderson G. L., Kaufman J. D. (2007). "Long-term exposure to air pollution and incidence of cardiovascular events in women.". *The New England Journal of Medicine* (Research Support, N.I.H., Extramural Research Support, U.S. Gov't, Non-P.H.S.) 356 (5): 447-458.

9

Impact of Air Pollution on Human Health

Prof. K. Venkata Rao

Introduction

"This work has broad potential public health implications," lead researcher Heather Volk said. "We've known for a long time that air pollution is bad for our lungs, and especially for children. We're now beginning to understand how air pollution may affect the brain."

The researchers estimated exposure to air pollution during each trimester of pregnancy and during the first year of life among 279 people with autism and 245 people without autism, all of whom were participants in the California-based Childhood Autism Risks from Genetics and the Environment (CHARGE) study. Exposure was calculated using addresses listed in residential histories and on the participants' birth certificates. The researchers then estimated regional air pollution levels using data from the *Environmental Protection Agencyís* (EPA) Air Quality System. The researchers then used air pollution data to calculate participants' exposure to three specific pollutants: nitrogen dioxide (NO_2), particulate matter fewer than 10 microns in diameter (PM_{10}), and particulate fewer than 2.5 microns in diameter ($PM_{2.5}$).

In addition, the researchers used dispersion models to calculate how much air pollution the participants had likely been exposed to by local traffic. The study is the first to look

* Deptt. of Commerce, Government College (A), Rajahmundry E.G. Distt., A.P.

at exposure not just to regional pollution, but also to that generated by local traffic. It follows a prior study by the same researchers that looked only at the correlation between autism risk and residence distance from a freeway.

We took into account how far away people lived from roads, meteorology such as which way the wind was blowing, how busy the road was, and other factors to study traffic-related pollution. We also examined data from air quality monitors, which measure pollution over a larger region that could come from traffic, industry, rail yards, or many other sources.

All Types of Pollution are Harmful

The researchers found that exposure to both local and regional air pollution - in any trimester of pregnancy or during the first year of life - significantly increased the risk of autism. Exposure to air pollution from local traffic more than doubled the risk of autism, while exposure to NO_2, PM10 or $PM_{2.5}$ from regional air pollution also increased the risk, even in the absence of local pollutants.

The finding that PM_{10} and $PM_{2.5}$ both increased risk was particularly interesting, the researchers noted, because prior studies have established that the finer $PM_{2.5}$ particles are more harmful to the body.

From studies conducted in the lab, we know that we can breathe in tiny particles and they can produce inflammation. Particles have varied composition, and there are many chemicals that can bind to them. The components of these particles could be hazardous to the brain.

Cleaning Up Commonly Found Air Pollutants

Six common air pollutants (also known as "criteria pollutants") are found all over the United States. They are particle pollution (often referred to as particulate matter), ground-level ozone, carbon monoxide, sulfur oxides, nitrogen oxides, and lead. These pollutants can harm your health and the environment, and cause property damage. Of the six pollutants, particle pollution and ground-level ozone are the most widespread health threats. Details about these two pollutants are discussed below. For information about the other common pollutants.

EPA calls these pollutants "criteria" air pollutants because it regulates them by developing human health based and/or environmentally-based criteria (science based guidelines) for setting permissible levels. The set of limits based on human health is called primary standards. Another set of limits intended to prevent environmental and property damage is called secondary standards. A geographic area with air quality that is cleaner than the primary standard is called an "attainment" area; areas that do not meet the primary standard are called "non-attainment" areas.

EPA has been developing programs to cut emissions of these commonly found air pollutants since the Clean Air Act was passed in 1970. It's a big job, and although a great deal of progress has been made, it will take time to make the air healthy throughout the country. For the latest information on air quality trends in the U.S. There are still several areas of the country, including many large cities, that are classified as non-attainment for at least one of the six common pollutants. Despite continued improvements in air quality, millions of people live in areas with monitoring data measuring unhealthy levels of pollution.

Particle Pollution

Particle pollution, also known as particulate matter (PM), includes the very fine dust, soot, smoke, and droplets that are formed from chemical reactions, and produced when fuels such as coal, wood, or oil are burned. For example, sulfur dioxide and nitrogen oxide gases from motor vehicles, electric power generation, and industrial facilities react with sunlight and water vapour to form particles. Particles may also come from fireplaces, wood stoves, unpaved roads, crushing and grinding operations, and may be blown into the air by the wind.

EPA scientists and other health experts are concerned about particle pollution because very small or "fine" particles can get deep into the lungs. These fine particles, by themselves, or in combination with other air pollutants, can cause increased emergency room visits and hospital admissions for respiratory illnesses, and tens of thousands of deaths each year. They can aggravate asthma, cause acute respiratory symptoms such as coughing, reduce lung function resulting in shortness of breath, and cause chronic bronchitis.

The elderly, children, and asthmatics are particularly susceptible to health problems caused by breathing fine particles. Individuals with pre-existing heart or lung disease are also at an increased risk of health problems due to particle pollution.

Particles also cause haze reducing visibility in places like national parks and wilderness areas that are known for their scenic vistas. These are places where we expect to see clearly for long distances. In many parts of the United States, pollution has reduced the distance and clarity of what we see by 70 percent.

Fine particles can remain suspended in the air and travel long distances with the wind. For example, over 20 per cent of the particles that form haze in the Rocky Mountains National Park have been estimated to come from hundreds of miles away.

Particles also make buildings, statues and other outdoor structures dirty. Trinity Church in downtown New York City was black until a few years ago, when cleaning off almost 200 years worth of soot brought the church's stone walls back to their original light pink colour.

Before the 1990 Clean Air Act went into effect, EPA set limits on airborne particles smaller than 10 micrometers in diameter called PM_{10}. These are tiny particles (seven of these particles lined up next to each other would cover a distance no wider than a human hair). Research has shown that even smaller particles (1/4 the size of a PM10 particle) are more likely to harm our health. So in 1997, EPA published limits for fine particles, called $PM_{2.5}$. To reduce particle levels, additional controls are being required on a variety of sources including power plants and diesel trucks.

Ground-level Ozone

Ground-level ozone is a primary component of smog. Ground-level ozone can cause human health problems and damage forests and agricultural crops. Repeated exposure to ozone can make people more susceptible to respiratory infections and lung inflammation. It also can aggravate pre-existing respiratory diseases, such as asthma. Children are at risk from ozone pollution because they are outside, playing and exercising, during the summer days when ozone levels are at their highest. They also can be more susceptible because their lungs are still developing. People with asthma and even active healthy adults, such as construction workers, can experience a reduction in lung function and an increase in respiratory symptoms (chest pain and coughing) when exposed to low levels of ozone during periods of moderate exertion.

The two types of chemicals that are the main ingredients in forming ground-level ozone are called volatile organic compounds (VOCs) and nitrogen oxides (NO_x). VOCs are released by cars burning gasoline, petroleum refineries, chemical manufacturing plants, and other industrial facilities. The solvents used in paints and other consumer and business products contain VOCs. The 1990 Clean Air Act has resulted in changes in product formulas to reduce the VOC content of those products. Nitrogen oxides (NO_x) are produced when cars and other sources like power plants and industrial boilers burn fuels such as gasoline, coal, or oil. The reddish-brown color you sometimes see when it is smoggy comes from the nitrogen oxides.

The pollutants that react to form ground-level ozone literally cook in the sky during the hot summer time season. It takes time for smog to form-several hours from the time pollutants get into the air until the ground-level ozone reaches unhealthy levels. For more information on days when air quality is expected to be unhealthy.

Weather and the lay of the land (for example, hills around a valley, high mountains between a big industrial city and suburban or rural areas) help determine where ground-level ozone goes and how bad it gets. When temperature inversions occur (warm air stays trapped near the ground by a layer of cooler air) and winds are calm, high concentrations of groundlevel ozone may persist for days at a time. As traffic and other sources add more ozone-forming pollutants to the air, the ground-level ozone gets worse.

How the Clean Air Act Reduces Air Pollution Such as Particle Pollution and Ground-level Ozone

First, EPA works with state governors and tribal government leaders to identify "non-attainment" areas where the air does not meet allowable limits for a common air pollutant. States and tribes usually do much of the planning for cleaning up common air pollutants. They develop plans, called State/ Tribal Implementation Plans, to reduce air pollutants to allowable levels. Then they use a permit system as part of their plan to make sure power plants, factories, and other pollution sources meet their goals to clean up the air.

The Clean Air Act requirements are comprehensive and cover many different pollution sources and a variety of clean-up methods to reduce common air pollutants. Many of the clean-up requirements for particle pollution and ground-level ozone involve large industrial sources (power plants, chemical producers, and petroleum refineries), as well as motor vehicles (cars, trucks, and buses). Also, in non-attainment areas, controls are generally required for smaller pollution sources, such as gasoline stations and paint shops.

What is Air Pollution?

Pollution is now a common place term, that our ears are attuned to. We hear about the various forms of pollution and read about it through the mass media. Air pollution is one such form that refers to the contamination of the air, irrespective of indoors or outside. A physical, biological or chemical alteration to the air in the atmosphere can be termed as pollution. It occurs when any harmful gases, dust, smoke enters into the atmosphere and makes it difficult for plants, animals and humans to survive as the air becomes dirty.

Air pollution can further be classified into two sections visible air pollution and invisible air pollution. Another way of looking at air pollution could be any substance that holds the potential to hinder the atmosphere or the well being of the living beings surviving in it. The sustainment of all things living is due to a combination of gases that collectively form the atmosphere; the imbalance caused by the increase or decrease of the percentage of these gases can be harmful for survival.

The ozone layer considered crucial for the existence of the ecosystems on the planet is depleting due to increased pollution. Global warning, a direct result of the increased imbalance of gases in the atmosphere has come to be known as the biggest threat and challenge that the contemporary world has to overcome in a bid for survival.

Types of Pollutants

In order to understand the causes of Air pollution, several divisions can be made. *Primarily air pollutants* can be caused by primary sources or secondary sources. The pollutants that are a direct result of the process can be called primary pollutants. A classic example of a primary pollutant would be the sulfur-dioxide emitted from factories

Secondary pollutants are the ones that are caused by the inter mingling and reactions of primary pollutants. Smog created by the interactions of several primary pollutants is known to be as secondary pollutant.

Causes of Air Pollution

- **Burning of fossil fuels:** Sulfur dioxide emitted from the combustion of fossil fuels like coal, petroleum and other factory combustibles is one the major cause of air pollution. Pollution emitting from vehicles including trucks, jeeps, cars, trains, airplanes cause immense amount of pollution. We rely on them to fulfil our daily basic needs of transportation. But, there overuse is killing our environment as dangerous gases are polluting the environment. Carbon Monooxide caused by improper or incomplete combustion and generally emitted from vehicles is another major pollutant along with Nitrogen Oxides, that is produced from both natural and man made processes.
- **Agricultural activities:** Ammonia is a very common by product from agriculture related activities and is one of the most hazardous gases in the atmosphere. Use of insecticides, pesticides and fertilizers in agricultural activities has grown quite a lot. They emit harmful chemicals into the air and can also cause water pollution.
- **Exhaust from factories and industries:** Manufacturing industries release large amount of carbon monoxide, hydrocarbons, organic compounds, and chemicals into the air thereby depleting the quality of air. Manufactu-

ring industries can be found at every corner of the earth and there is no area that has not been affected by it. Petroleum refineries also release hydrocarbons and various other chemicals that pollute the air and also cause land pollution.

- **Mining operations:** Mining is a process wherein minerals below the earth are extracted using large equipments. During the process dust and chemicals are released in the air causing massive air pollution. This is one of the reason which is responsible for the deteriorating health conditions of workers and nearby residents.
- **Indoor air pollution:** Household cleaning products, painting supplies emit toxic chemicals in the air and cause air pollution. Have you ever noticed that once you paint walls of your house, it creates some sort of smell which makes it literally impossible for you to breathe.

Suspended particulate matter (SPM) popular by its acronym SPM, is another cause of pollution. Referring to the particles afloat in the air, SPM is usually caused by dust, combustion etc.

Effects of Air Pollution

- **Respiratory and heart problems:** The effects of Air pollution are alarming. They are known to create several respiratory and heart conditions along with Cancer, among other threats to the body. Several millions are known to have died due to direct or indirect effects of Air pollution. Children in areas exposed to air pollutants are said to commonly suffer from pneumonia and asthma.
- **Global warming:** Another direct effect is the immediate alterations that the world is witnessing due to Global warming. With increased temperatures world wide, increase in sea levels and melting of ice from colder regions and icebergs, displacement and loss of

habitat have already signaled an impending disaster if actions for preservation and normalization aren't undertaken soon.

- **Acid Rain:** Harmful gases such as nitrogen oxides and sulfur oxides are released into the atmosphere during the burning of fossil fuels. When it rains, the water droplets combines with these air pollutants, becomes acidic and then falls on the ground in the form of acid rain. Acid rain can cause great damage to human, animals and crops.
- **Eutrophication:** Eutrophication is a condition where high amount of nitrogen present in some pollutants gets developed on sea's surface and turns itself into algae and adversely affect fish, plants and animal species. The green colored algae that is present on lakes and ponds is due to presence of this chemical only.
- **Effect on Wildlife:** Just like humans, animals also face some devastating affects of air pollution. Toxic chemicals present in the air can force wildlife species to move to new place and change their habitat. The toxic pollutants deposit over the surface of the water and can also affect sea animals.
- **Depletion of ozone layer:** Ozone exists in earth's stratosphere and is responsible for protecting humans from harmful ultraviolet (UV) rays. Earth's ozone layer is depleting due to the presence of chlorofluorocarbons, hydro chloro-fluorocarbons in the atmosphere. As ozone layer will go thin, it will emit harmful rays back on earth and can cause skin and eye related problems. UV rays also have the capability to affect crops.

When you try to study the sources of air pollution, you enlist a series of activities and interactions that create these pollutants. There are two types of sources that we will take a look at: *Natural sources and Man-made sources.*

Natural Sources of Pollution

Natural sources of pollution include dust carried by the wind from locations with very little or no green cover, gases released from the body processes of living beings (Carbon dioxide from humans during respiration, Methane from cattle during digestion, Oxygen from plants during Photosynthesis). Smoke from the combustion of various inflammable objects, volcanic eruptions etc along with the emission of polluted gases also make it to the list of Natural sources of Pollution.

Man-made Sources of Pollution

While looking at the man-made contributions towards air pollution, smoke again features as a prominent component. The smoke emitted from various forms of combustion like in bio mass, factories, vehicles, furnaces etc. Waste used to create landfills generate methane, that is harmful in several ways. The reactions of certain gases and chemicals also form harmful fumes that can be dangerous to the well being of living creatures.

Solutions for Air Pollution

- **Use public mode of transportation:** Encourage people to use more and more public modes of transportation to reduce pollution. Also, try to make use of car pooling. If you and your colleagues come from the same locality and have same timings you can explore this option to save energy and money.
- **Conserve energy:** Switch off fans and lights when you are going out. Large amount of fossil fuels are burnt to produce electricity. You can save the environment from degradation by reducing the amount of fossil fuels to be burned.
- **Understand the concept of Reduce, Reuse and Recycle:** Do not throw away items that are of no use to you. In-fact reuse them for some other purpose, *e.g.*, you can use old jars to store cereals or pulses.
- **Emphasis on clean energy resources:** Clean energy technologies like solar, wind and geothermal are on high these days. Governments of various countries have been providing grants to consumers who are interested

in installing solar panels for their home. This will go a long way to curb air pollution.

- **Use energy efficient devices:** CFL lights consume less electricity as against their counterparts. They live longer, consume less electricity, lower electricity bills and also help you to reduce pollution by consuming less energy.

Several attempts are being made world wide on a personal, industrial and governmental levels to curb the intensity at which Air Pollution is rising and regain a balance as far as the proportions of the foundation gases are concerned. This is a direct attempt at slacking Global warming. We are seeing a series of innovations and experiments aimed at alternate and unconventional options to reduce pollutants. Air Pollution is one of the larger mirrors of man's follies, and a challenge we need to overcome to see a tomorrow.

REFERENCES

Andersen, Z. J., Hvidberg, M., Jensen, S. S., Ketzel, M., Loft, S., Sorensen, M., and Raaschou-Nielsen, O. (2011). Chronic obstructive pulmonary disease and long-term exposure to traffic-related air pollution: a cohort study. [Research Support, Non-U.S. Gov't]. *American journal of respiratory and critical care medicine*, 183(4), 455-461.

Gehring, U., Wijga, A. H., Brauer, M., Fischer, P., de Jongste, J. C., Kerkhof, M., and Brunekreef, B. (2010). Traffic-related air pollution and the development of asthma and allergies during the first 8 years of life. [Research Support, Non-U.S. Gov't]. *American journal of respiratory and critical care medicine*, 181(6), 596-603.

Health effects of outdoor air pollution. Committee of the Environmental and Occupational Health Assembly of the American Thoracic Society. (1996). [Comparative Study Review]. *American journal of respiratory and critical care medicine*, 153(1), 3-50.

Michael Kymisis, and Konstantinos Hadjistavrou (2008). "Short-Term Effects of Air Pollution Levels on Pulmonary Function of Young Adults". *The Internet Journal of Pulmonary Medicine 9 (2).*

Zoidis, John D. (1999). "The Impact of Air Pollution on COPD". *RT: for Decision Makers in Respiratory Care.*

10

Air Pollution and Health Hazards

(Dr.) Prof. R.P. Sarma

Introduction

Growth of an economy brings more comfortable living with developed equipments and faster travelling system but at the same time it brings in many hazards with it, which makes living more dangerous to live. Economic development get higher GDP, at the same time it also brings with it another GDP, which is Gross Domestic Pollution (GDPL) economists and social scientists so far mainly concerned with GDP but now when GDPL grows with GDP it is now a Herculean task for the economists to control it. Even though GDPL cannot be control fully but it can be controlled partially and preventive measures can be taken to minimize it for comfortable life in the world.

Pollution comes from several sources: air, water, sound, light and simply growth of population. An individual is affected by these pollutants some times without knowledge. Here we would discuss about the pollution created through air, which is one of the main causes of total pollutions in an area. There are various locations, activities or factors which are responsible for releasing pollutants into the atmosphere.

These sources can be classified into two major categories. (1) Man-made Sources and (2) Natural Sources.

* Director, Institute of Economic Studies, Brahmapur–10.

Man-made Sources

These are mostly related to the burning of multiple types of fuel. Here also there are several categories of sources:

1. **Stationary Sources** include smoke stacks of power plants, manufacturing facilities (factories) arid waste incinerators, as well as furnaces and other types of fuel-burning heating devices. In developing and poor countries, traditional biomass burning is the major source of air pollutants; traditional biomass includes wood, crop waste and dung. Mobile Sources include motor vehicles, marine vessels, and aircraft.
2. **Chemicals**, dust and controlled burn practices in agriculture and forest management. Controlled or prescribed burning is a technique sometimes used in forest management, farming, prairie restoration or greenhouse gas abatement. Fire is a natural part of both forest and grassland ecology and controlled fire can be a tool for foresters. Controlled burning stimulates the germination of some desirable forest trees, thus renewing me forest.
3. Fumes from paint, hair spray, varnish, aerosol sprays and other solvents.
4. Waste deposition in landfills, which generate methane. Methane is highly flammable and may form explosive mixtures with air. Methane is also an asphyxiate and may displace oxygen in an enclosed space. Asphyxia or suffocation may result if the oxygen concentration is reduced to below 19.5 per cent by displacement.
5. Military resources, such as nuclear weapons, toxic gases, germ warfare and rocketry.

Natural Sources

1. Dust from natural sources, usually large areas of land with few or no vegetation.
2. Methane, emitted by the digestion of food by animals, for example cattle.

3. Radon gas from radioactive decay within the Earth's crust. Radon is a colorless, odorless, naturally occurring, radioactive noble gas that is formed from the decay of radium. It is considered to be a health hazard. Radon gas from natural sources can accumulate in buildings, especially in confined areas such as the basement and it is the second most frequent cause of lung cancer, after cigarette smoking.
4. Smoke and carbon monoxide from wildfires.
5. Vegetation, in some regions, emits environmentally significant amounts of VOCs on warmer days. These VOCs react with primary anthropogenic pollutants—specifically, NO_x, SO_2, and anthropogenic organic carbon compounds—to produce a seasonal haze of secondary pollutants.
6. Volcanic activity, which produces sulfur, chlorine, and ash particulates.

Health Hazards

Air pollution risk is a function of the hazard of the pollutant and the exposure to that pollutant. Air pollution exposure can be expressed for an individual, for certain groups, or for entire populations. For example, one may want to calculate the exposure to a hazardous air pollutant for a geographic area, which includes the various microenvironments and age groups. This can be calculated as an inhalation exposure. This would account for daily exposure in various settings (*e.g.* different indoor micro-environments and outdoor locations). The exposure needs to include different age and other demographic groups, especially infants, children, pregnant women and other sensitive subpopulations.

The exposure to an air pollutant must integrate the concentrations of the air pollutant with respect to the time spent in each setting and the respective inhalation rates for each subgroup for each specific time that the subgroup is in the setting and engaged in particular activities that is, playing, cooking, reading, working, etc. For example, a small child's inhalation rate will be less than that of an adult. A child engaged in vigorous exercise will have a higher respiration rate than the same child in a sedentary activity. The daily exposure, then, needs to reflect the time spent in each micro-environmental setting and the type of activities in these settings. The air pollutant concentration in each micro activity/ micro environmental setting is summed to indicate the exposure.

Air pollution is a significant risk factor for multiple health conditions including respiratory infections, heart disease, and lung cancer, according to the WHO. The health effects caused by air pollution may include difficulty in breathing, wheezing, coughing, asthma and aggravation of existing respiratory and cardiac conditions. These effects can result in increased medication use, increased doctor or emergency room visits, more hospital admissions and, premature death. The human health effects of poor air quality are far reaching, but principally affect the body's respiratory system and the cardiovascular system. Individual reactions to air pollutants depend on the type of pollutant a person is exposed to, the degree of exposure, the individual's health status and genetics. The most common sources of air pollution include particulates, ozone, nitrogen dioxide, and sulfur dioxide. Both indoor and outdoor air pollution have caused approximately 3.3 million deaths worldwide. Children aged less than five years that live in developing countries are the most vulnerable population in terms of total deaths attributable to indoor and outdoor air pollution.

According to the World Health Organization 2.4 million people die each year from causes directly attributable to air pollution, with 1.5 million of these deaths attributable to indoor air pollution. "Epidemiological studies suggest that more than 500,000 Americans die each year from cardiopulmonary disease linked to breathing fine particle air pollution. A study by the University of Birmingham has shown a strong correlation between pneumonia related deaths and aim pollution from motor vehicles. Worldwide more deaths per year are linked to air pollution than to automobile accidents. A 2005 study by the European Commission calculated that air pollution reduces life expectancy by an average of almost nine months across the European Union. Causes of deaths include aggravated asthma, emphysema, lung and heart diseases, and respiratory allergies. In The USA EPA estimates that'a proposed set of changes in diesel engine technology (Tier 2) could result in 12,000 fewer premature mortalities, 15,000 fewer heart attacks, 6,000 fewer emergency room visits by children with asthma, and 8,900 fewer respiratory-related hospital admissions each year in the United States.

In India

The worst short term civilian pollution crisis in India was the 1984 Bhopal Disaster. Leaked industrial vapours from the Union Carbide factory, belonging to Union Carbide, Inc., U.S.A. (later bought over by Dow Chemical Company), killed more than 25,000 people outright and injured anywhere from 150,000 to 600,000. The United Kingdom suffered its worst air pollution event when the December 4 Great Smog of 1952 formed over London. In six days more than 4,000 died, and 8,000 more died within the following months.

Diesel exhaust is a major contributor to combustion derived particulate matter air pollution. In several human experimental studies, using a well validated exposure chamber setup, DE has been linked to acute vascular dysfunction and increased thrombus formation. This serves as a plausible mechanistic link between the previously described association between particulates air pollution and increased cardiovascular morbidity and mortality.

Effects on Cardiovascular Health

A 2007 review of evidence found ambient air pollution exposure is a risk factor correlating with increased total mortality from cardiovascular events. Air pollution is also emerging as a risk factor for stroke, particularly in developing countries where pollutant levels are highest. A 2007 study found that in women air pollution is associated not with hemorrhagic but with ischemic stroked Air pollution was also found to be associated with increased incidence and mortality from coronary stroke in a cohort study in 2011. Associations are believed to be causal and effects may be mediated by vasoconstriction, low-grade inflammation or autonomic nervous system imbalance or other mechanisms.

Effects on Cystic Fibrosis

A study from around the years of 1999 to 2000, by the University of Washington, showed that patients near and around particulates air pollution had an increased risk of pulmonary exacerbations and decrease in lung function. Patients were examined before the study for amounts of specific pollutants like Pseudomonas aeruginosa or Burkholderia cenocepacia as well as their socioeconomic standing. Participants involved in the study were located in the United States in close proximity to an Environmental Protection Agency. During the time of the study 117 deaths were associated with air pollution. Many patients in the study lived in or near large metropolitan areas in order to be close to medical help. These same patients had higher level of pollutants found in their system because of more emissions in larger cities. As cystic fibrosis patients already suffer from decreased lung function, everyday pollutants such as smoke, emissions from automobiles, tobacco smoke and improper use of indoor heating devices could further compromise lung function.

Effects on COPD and Asthma

Chronic obstructive pulmonary disease (COPD) includes diseases such as chronic bronchitis and emphysema.

Researchers have demonstrated increased risk of developing asthma and COPD from increased 'exposure' to traffic-related air pollution. Additionally, air pollution has been associated with increased hospitalizations and mortality from asthma and COPD. A study conducted in 1960-1961 in the wake of the Great Smog of 1952 compared 293 London residents with 477 residents of Gloucester, Peterborough, and Norwich, three towns with low reported death rates from chronic bronchitis. All subjects were male postal truck drivers aged 40 to 59. Compared to the subjects from the outlying towns, the London subjects exhibited more severe respiratory symptoms (including cough, phlegm, and dispread), reduced lung function and peak flow rate), and increased sputum production and purulence. The differences were more pronounced for subjects aged 50 to 59. The study controlled for age and smoking habits, so concluded that air pollution was the most likely cause of the observed differences. It is believed that much like cystic fibrosis, by living in a more urban environment serious health hazards become more apparent. Studies have shown that in urban areas patients suffer mucus hyper secretion, lower levels of lung function, and more self diagnosis of chronic bronchitis and emphysema.

Causes for Cancer

A review of evidence regarding whether ambient air pollution exposure is a risk factor for cancer in 2007 found solid data to conclude that long-term exposure to $PM_{2.5}$ (fine particulates) increases the overall risk of non-accidental mortality by 6 per cent per a 10 micro g/m^3 increase. Exposure to $PM_{2.5}$ was also associated with an increased risk of mortality from lung cancer (range: 15% to 21% per a 10 microg/m^3 increase) and total cardiovascular mortality (range: 12% to 14% per a 10 microg/m^3 increase). The review further noted that living close to busy traffic appears to be associated with elevated risks of these three outcomes increase in lung cancer deaths, cardiovascular deaths, and overall non-accidental deaths. The reviewers also found suggestive evidence that exposure to $PM_{2.5}$ is positively associated with mortality from coronary heart diseases and exposure to SO_2 increases mortality from lung cancer, but the data was insufficient to provide solid conclusions. In 2011, a large Danish epidemiological study found an increased risk of lung cancer for patients who lived in areas with high nitrogen oxide concentrations. In this study, the association was higher for non-smokers than smokers. An additional Danish study, also in 2011, likewise noted evidence of possible associations between air pollution and other forms of cancer, including cervical cancer and brain cancer.

Effects on Children

Around the world, children living in cities with high exposure to air pollutants are at increased risk of developing asthma, pneumonia and other lower respiratory infections. Air pollution is also a significant contribution to environmental toxins in pregnancy. The World Health Organization reports that the greatest concentrations of participates are found in countries with low economic world power and high poverty and population growth rates. Examples of these countries include Egypt, Sudan, Mongolia, and Indonesia. However, even in the United States, despite the passage of the Clean Air Act in 1970, in 2002 at least 146 million Americans were living in non-attainment areas—regions in which the concentration of certain air pollutants exceeded federal standards. These dangerous pollutants are known as the criteria pollutants, and include ozone, particulates, sulfur dioxide, nitrogen dioxide, carbon monoxide, and lead. Protective measures to ensure children's health are being taken in cities such as New Delhi, India where buses now use compressed natural gas to help eliminate the "pea-soup" smog.

In Clean Areas

Even in the areas with relatively low levels of air pollution, public health effects can be significant and costly, since a large number of people breathe in such pollutants. A 2005 scientific study for the British Columbia Lung Association showed that a small improvement in air quality (1% reduction of ambient $PM_{2.5}$ and ozone concentrations) would produce a $29 million in animal 'saving's in the Metro Vancouver region in 2010 This finding is based on health valuation of lethal (death) and sub-lethal (illness) affects.

How to Reduce Pollution?

There are various air pollution control technologies and land use planning strategies available to reduce air pollution At its most basic level land use planning is likely to involve zoning and transport infrastructure planning. In most developed countries, land-use planning is an important part of social policy, ensuring that land is used efficiently for the benefit of the wider economy and population as well as to protect the environment. Efforts to reduce pollution from mobile sources includes primary regulation (many developing countries have permissive regulations), expanding regulation to new sources (such as cruise and transport ships, farm equipment, and small gas-powered equipment such as lawn trimmers, chainsaws, and snowmobiles, increased fuel efficiency (such as through the use of hybrid vehicles), conversion to cleaner fuels (such as bioethanol, biodiesel, or conversion to electric vehicles). Titanium dioxide has been researched for it's ability to reduce air pollution. Ultra violet light will release free electrons from the material creating free radicals, breaking up VOCs and NO_x gases. One form is super hydrophilic.

Control Devices

The following items are commonly used as pollution control devices by industry or transportation devices. They can either destroy contaminants or remove them from an exhaust stream before it is emitted into the atmosphere.

Participate Control

- Mechanical collectors (dust cyclones, multicyclones)
- **Electrostatic precipitators:** An electrostatic precipitator (ESP), or electrostatic air cleaner is a particulate collection device that removes particles from a flowing gas (such as air) using the force of an induced electrostatic charge. Electrostatic precipitators are highly efficient filtration devices that minimally impede the flow of gases through the device, and can easily remove fine participates such as dust and smoke from the air stream.
- **Baghouses:** Designed to handle heavy dust loads, a dust collector consists of a blower, dust filter, a filter-cleaning system, and a dust receptacle or dust removal system (distinguished from air cleaners which utilize disposable filters to remove the dust).
- **Particulate scrubbers:** Wet scrubber is a form of pollution control technology. The term describes a variety of devices that use pollutants from a furnace flue gas or from other gas streams. In a wet scrubber, the polluted gas stream is brought into contact with the scrubbing liquid, by spraying it with the liquid, by forcing it through a pool of liquid, or by some other contact method, so as to remove the pollutants.

Environmentalists advise for people's activities according to the to the Air Health Index which is tabulated in Table 10.1.

If the Air Health Index (AHI) is below 4 health risks is very low, one can enjoy outdoor activities without any fear. But if AHI is above 10 one has to reduce strenuous activates outside to prevent health hazards.

Table 10.1 : People's Ideal Activity According to Air Health Index

Health Risk	Air Quality Health Index	What you have to do	Your Activities
Low	1-3	Enjoy your usual out door activities	Ideal air quality for outdoor activities
Moderate	4-6	Consider reducing or rescheduling strenuous activities outdoors if you are experiencing symptoms.	No need to modify your usual outdoor activities unless you experience symptoms such as coughing and throat irritation.
High	7-10	Reduce or reschedule strenuous activities outdoors. Children and the elderly should also take it easy.	Consider reducing or rescheduling strenuous activities outdoors if you experience symptoms such as coughing and throat irritation.
Very High	> 10	Avoid strenuous activities outdoors. Children, and the elderly should alsoavoid outdoor physical exertion.	Reduce or reschedule strenuous activities outdoors, especially if you experience symptoms such as coughing and throat irritation.

Urban Hazards

Air pollution mainly affects in urban areas, and as world is moving fast in urbanization the hazard have to be faced more and more in cities and towns in comparison to rural areas. Survey of cities world-wide for air pollution in 2004 shows top eight cities according to air pollution seven are in Asia, of which four in India. Delhi is the second position air pollution in the world after Cairo.

Air Pollution Index and cities are shown in Table 10.2.

Table 10.2 : Air Pollution in the Cities, 2004

Sl.No.	Mg/m^3	City	Country
1.	168	Cairo	Egypt
2.	150	Delhi	India
3.	128	Kolkata	India
4.	125	Tianjini	China
5.	123	Chongoing	China
6.	109	Kanpur	India
7.	104	Lucknow	India
8.	101	Shenyang	China

Conclusion

Pollution in the society created from several sources. Air pollution is one of the important pollution that creates several health hazards for people and makes the life miserable. Deaths from air pollutions reported from all over the world over that is in increasing trend. It affects on cardiovascular health, effects on cystic fibrosis and also causes for Cancer around the world. Children living in cities with high exposure to air pollutants are at increased risk of developing asthma, pneumonia and other lower respiratory infections. In clean areas also air pollution, public health effects can be significant and costly, since a large number of people breathe in such pollutants. Air pollution cannot be fully eliminated but measures taken to prevent air pollution would lead to an healthier life in the world.

REFERENCES

"Air pollution causes early deaths". BBC. February 21, 2005.

Collins, Nick (April 18,2012). "Exhaust fumes are twice as deadly as roads, study claims". *The Telegraph*.

Daniel A. Vallero. *Fundamentals of Air Pollution*. Elsevier Academic Press.

Duflo, E., Greenstone, M., and Hanna, R. (2008) "Indoor air pollution, health and economic well-being"; "S.A.P.I.EN.S." '''1''' (1)". Sapiens.revues.org.

"EMEP/EEA air pollutant emission inventory guidebook—2009". Eea.europa.eu. 2009-06-19.

"Environmental Pollution" Theenvironmentalblogiorg. 2011-12-16.

Evidence growing of air pollution's link to heart disease, death// American Heart Association. May 10, 2010.

"Estimated deaths and DALYs attributable to selected environmental risk factors, by WHO Member State, 2002".

Goldstein, Alien H., Charles D. Koven, Colette L. Heald, Inez Y. Fung (2009-05-05). "Biogenic carbon and anthropogenic pollutants combine to form a cooling haze over the south-eastern United States". *Proceedings of the National Academy of Sciences.*

"How Can Air Pollution Hurt My Health?". *Health Effects of Air Pollution.* Lawrence Berkeley National Laboratory, US Department of Energy.

"Infant Inhalation of Ultrafine Air Pollution Linked to Adult Lung Disease". Sciencedaily.com. 2009-07-23.

"Newly detected air pollutant mimics damaging effects of cigarette smoke"

"Newly detected air pollutant mimics damaging effects of cigarette smoke", www.eurekalert.org. Archived from the original on 28 August 2008.

"Reports". WorstPolluted.org. Archived from the original on 11 August 2010.

"Revised 1996 IPCC Guidelines for National Greenhouse Gas Inventories (reference manual)".

"Study links traffic pollution to thousands of deaths". *The Guardian* (London, UK: Guardian Media Group). 2008-04-15. Archived from the original on 20 April 2008.

Tankersley, Jim (January 8, 2010). "EPA proposes nation's strictest smog limits ever". Los Angeles Times.

"United Kingdom's emission factor database". Naei.org.uk.

11

Impact of Air Pollution on Human Brain and Physical Changes

K. Harerama Krishna*
Dr. R.N. Misra**

Introduction

No one likes breathing polluted air. Exhaust fumes and particulate matter hanging in the air can make you cough and give you a headache. As *Natural News* has reported previously, it can harm your health in ways that aren't so obvious, as well. Now comes information from another Ohio State University study that long-term exposure to air pollution can literally change your brain. And as you might expect, these physical changes in the brain are not beneficial. They are associated with learning and memory problems and even depression.

The new study, just published online in the journal *Molecular Psychiatry* is the first long-term research to show the negative impact of air pollution on the brain, according to Laura Fonken, lead author of the study and a doctoral student in neuroscience at Ohio State University. "The results suggest prolonged exposure to polluted air can have visible, negative effects on the brain, which can lead to a variety of health problems," Fonken said in a statement to the media.

* Deptt. of Commerce, Government College (A), Rajahmundry E.G. Distt., A.P.

** Prof. (MBA) Retd. Government College (A), Rajahmundry E.G. Distt., A.P.

In earlier studies in mice, researchers in Ohio State University's Davis Heart and Lung Research Institute (who also collaborated with Fonken and colleagues on the new research project) found that fine air particulate matter causes widespread inflammation in the body leading to a heightened risk for diabetes and obesity, as well as hypertension. Their extended research on air pollution's impact on the brain adds more disturbing evidence that bad air is bad for thinking, too.

"The more we learn about the health effects of prolonged exposure to air pollution, the more reasons there are to be concerned," stated Randy Nelson, co-author of the study and professor of neuroscience and psychology at Ohio State, in the press statement.

For the new study, lab mice were exposed five days a week to either filtered air or polluted air for six hours a day. The polluted air contained the same type of pollution created by cars, factories and natural dust and included very fine particulate matter—particles so minute they are only about 1/30th of the average width of a human hair. Because of their small size, these particles can be inhaled deeply into the lungs and end up in other organs of the body.

The mice were exposed to an amount of polluted air equivalent to what people are exposed to in some polluted urban areas, according to the researchers. Then various behavioral tests were performed on the rodents after the animals spent 10 months regularly breathing either filtered or polluted air.

The results showed severe impairments in memory and learning in the pollution exposed animals. And mice exposed to the polluted air exhibited more depressive-like behaviors than did the mice that breathed the clean air. In addition, the polluted-air breathing mice showed signs of higher levels of anxiety-like behaviours in one specific test, but not in another.

So how could air pollution trigger changes in learning, memory and mood? To find out, the scientists focused on the hippocampus, the area of the brain associated with learning, memory and depression.

The results? The researchers found undeniable physical differences in the hippocampi of the mice who were exposed to polluted air compared to the animals who breathed clean air. Specifically, neurons (nerve cells) known as dendrites were clearly changed. Normally, dendrites have small projections growing off them, dubbed spines, which transmit signals from one neuron to another. But in the mice exposed to polluted air, there were shorter dendrites, fewer dendrite spikes and, overall, a reduction in the complexity of brain cells. And earlier research has shown that these types of changes are linked to decreased learning and memory abilities.

The research team found evidence that low-grade inflammation was evident in the hippocampus in the pollution exposed mice. That could have caused the brain changes. Inflammation-causing chemical messengers in the immune system known as cytokines were found to be more active in the hippocampus in the animals who breathed the polluted air.

"The hippocampus is particularly sensitive to damage caused by inflammation," Fonken said in the media statement. "We suspect that the systemic inflammation caused by breathing polluted air is being communicated to the central nervous system."

Although the new study involved mice and not humans, the scientists think the findings have profound implications for people exposed regularly to air pollution. *ìThis could have importantíí.*

Where can We Come in Contact with Air Pollutants

Air is one of the most important substances for humans, together with water. To survive, humans need oxygen. We breathe air every day and consequentially it is very important that the air around us is clean. Air pollutants can cause health problems when we breathe them in.

In the past century we have performed very extensive research to bring to light the health and environmental effects of air pollutants. This research has provided us with a lot of information. We now know, for example, that people that live near highways or industrial areas are more susceptible to diseases such as cancer and asthma. This may increase their chances to an earlier death.

People may not only come in contact with air pollutants when they are outside, in the workplace environment, people may come in contact with air pollutants as well. This is likely to happen to people that work with dangerous chemicals, but it can also happen to people in offices. In the office the air that is circulated through the ventilation system may be contaminated with pathogenic microorganisms.

At home the air can be contaminated with all kinds of chemicals that may be damaging to our health. These contaminants can come from household equipment, such as carpets and curtains. Carpets and curtains can cause bromines to end up in indoor air, which is a 'carcinogen'. Carcinogens are contaminants that can cause cancer.

Indoor air may also be contaminated with microorganisms, which are known to cause all kinds of rashes and allergies. When a house is not properly aerated, contaminants may accumulate in the indoor air.

What are the Health Effects of Air Pollutants on Humans?

Air pollutants usually act upon the respiratory tract, first. Air pollutants can enter a human body through several entranceways, such as the skin, mouth and lungs. Gaseous pollutants can deeply penetrate the respiratory system and absorb on wet body tissues on the way. This may cause the pH of the body fluids to change, causing irritations. Organic solvents can easily be absorbed by blood, transporting them through the entire body rapidly.

The chances of penetration of a human body by contaminants mainly depend upon the size of the particles. Larger particles stay behind in the nose or are swallowed, but smaller particles can penetrate the lungs. Smaller particles absorb more toxic material, which they can take deeper into the body. When contaminants are water-soluble, they can immediately be absorbed by human blood.

What Health Effects do Air Pollutants have on Animals?

The health effects that pollutants cause with animals are similar to the health effects they cause with humans. However, there are some effects that do not occur with humans. For example, acid rain can cause serious health effects for water organisms, such as reproduction failure, or even death.

What Health Effects do Air Pollutants have on Plants?

Plants are much more susceptible for gaseous air pollutants than humans and animals. Examples of gaseous air pollutants are hydrogen fluoride (HF), ozone (O_3) and ethene. Air pollutants mainly penetrate a plant through skin pores. These are in connection with the intercellular spaces in the leaves of a plant. Through the skin pores gasses can penetrate cell walls, to be absorbed by the cell fluids. Some of the gaseous air pollutants directly damage plant leaves when they penetrate plant cells. This can cause the leaves of plants and trees to lose their colour, or even die off. It can also cause plant growth to stagnate. The leaves and stems may slacken and curl up.

In some cases however, a plant can restore itself after fresh air is added to its location.

What are Specific Health Effects of Air Pollutants

Health effects of air pollutants do not occur until a certain dose has penetrated a plant, animal or human body. This dose differs for each air pollutant. When the concentrations of air pollutants increase, the risk of health effects will be higher.

Air pollutants can cause acute effects, such as coughing and throat pains, but there are air pollutants that only cause cronic effects, such as asbestos. Here, we will sum up some commonly known air pollutants and give a brief description of their health effects.

Carbon Monoxide (CO)

Carbon monoxide is a gas that is absorbed by haemoglobin in the blood after it has entered a human body, causing the blood to be less able to transport oxygen.

When carbon monoxide is absorbed in low concentrations, people will experience tiredness. People that have heart conditions often experience chest pains. Higher concentrations of carbon monoxide cause bad vision, decreases in concentration, headaches, dizziness, nausea and confusion. When carbon monoxide concentrations are very high, it can be mortal.

Carbon monoxide is likely to fashion during incomplete combustion. To prevent the fashioning of carbon monoxide in your house, you may want to clean your chimneys and heaters once a year. It is also recommended to have water heaters checked out.

Sulphur Dioxide (SO_2)

The effects of sulphur dioxide mainly take place when it is converted to sulphuric acids. This acid has some negative effects on the respiratory tract. Sulphur dioxide is fashioned during fossil fuel combustion.

Ozone (O_3)

Ozone causes mucous membrane irritation, respiratory infections and lung infections. Ozone consists during thunderstorms, through electrolyses of oxygen. Ozone is generated through the same principle. Ozone is also shaped in traffic. It exists naturally in the atmosphere, under the influence of UV-radiation.

Nitrogen Oxides (NO_3)

The health effects of nitrogen oxides are similar to those caused by ozone. However, health effects of nitrogen oxides only occur when higher concentrations are absorbed. Nitrogen oxides are fashioned during high-temperature combustion.

Asbestos

Asbestos has no acute health effects. Long-term exposure to asbestos can cause breast, peritoneum and lung cancer, along with various lung infections. Asbestos is a very persistent contaminant, it is hardly biologically degradable and it can withstand heat, acids and basics. This makes asbestos suitable for many different applications. Due to the fact that asbestos is a carcinogen, it is now banned from all applications in many countries.

Lead (Pb)

Cars that use lead-containing gasoline, will emit lead. High lead concentrations in air can cause disturbances in physical and mental development of children. Lead is commonly known to cause a decrease in coordination and mental capacities, as well as kidney damage, damage to the nervous system and a lack in red blood cells.

Benzene

Benzene is a carcinogenic contaminant. It causes leukaemia.

PAH's (Poly Aromatic Hydrocarbons)

PAH's are potentially carcinogenic contaminants. They are fashioned during several industrial processes and they are emitted by traffic.

Cigarette Smoke

Cigarette smoke can cause mucous membrane irritation, eye, nose and respiratory infections, bronchitis and lung cancer.

Hydrocarbons

Hydrocarbons cause mucous membrane irritations, headaches, a loss of coordination, nausea and liver damage. Some hydrocarbons are potentially carcinogenic to humans, as well as animals.

REFERENCES

"Air pollution causes early deaths". BBC. February 21, 2005.

"AP 42, Volume I". Epa.gov. Archived from the original on 24 September 2010.

Collins, Nick (April 18, 2012). "Exhaust fumes are twice as deadly as roads, study claims". The Telegraph.

David Pennise and Kirk Smith. "Biomass Pollution Basics". WHO.

Evidence growing of air pollution's link to heart disease, death// American Heart Association, May 10, 2010.

"EMEP/EEA air pollutant emission inventory guidebook—2009". Eea.europa.eu. 2009-06-19.

"Environmental Pollution". The environmental blog.org. 2011-12-16.

"Estimated deaths & DALYs attributable to selected environmental risk factors, by WHO Member State, 2002".

Goldstein, Alien H., Charles D. Koven, Colette L. Heald and Inez Y. Fung (2009-05-05). "Biogenic carbon and anthropogenic pollutants combine to form a cooling haze over the south-eastern United States". *Proceedings of the National Academy of Sciences.*

"Indoor air pollution and household energy". WHO and UNEP. 2011.

Mr Chen's claim was made in The Lancet (December 2013 issue) and reported in The Daily Telegraph 8th January 2014 page 15 'Air pollution killing up to 500,000 Chinese each year, admits former health minister.

"Newly detected air pollutant mimics damaging effects of cigarette smoke".

"Newly detected air pollutant mimics damaging effects of cigarette smoke", www.eurekalert.org. Archived from the original on 28 August 2008.

"Infant Inhalation of Ultrafine Air Pollution Linked To Adult Lung Disease". Sciencedaily.com. 2009-07-23.

"Revised 1996 IPCC Guidelines for National Greenhouse Gas Inventories (reference manual)". Ipcc-nggip.iges.or.jp.

"Study links traffic pollution to thousands of deaths". *The Guardian* (London, UK: Guardian Media Group). 2008-04-15. Archived from the original on 20 April 2008.

"United Kingdom's emission factor database". Naei.org.uk.

12

Air Pollution and Development

Dr. B. Eswar Rao Patnaik*

Introduction

The present chapter is an effort to discuss the nature, causes and effects of air pollution on society. The paper also offers a set of policy measures for containing air pollution. The academic work is based on secondary data. The concept and causes of air pollution are depicted, The magnitude and adverse effects of air pollution on society and surroundings of the country and a trip on action oriented programme and government policies to combat the menace of air pollution are presented in this chapter. Who has defined air pollution as "the presence in air of substances put there by acts of man in concentration sufficient to interfere with the comfort, safety or health of man or with the full use or enjoyment of his property". The presence of contaminants in the atmosphere is considered to be in sufficient quantities and duration, to cause them to be injurious to human health animal and plant life and reduce welfare in general.

Ecological imbalance embodied in air pollution is caused by natural sources and man-made sources. Volcanic eruptions, forest fires caused, by the practice of shifting cultivation, dust storms and pollen grains of flowers are natural sources of air pollution. Man-nature interaction results in air pollution. Natural resources, whether renewable or non-renewable are

* Principal, S.B.R.G. Women's Government College, Berhampur-1, Odisha.

scarce in a country and hence demands productive use of these precious resources. The consideration of future generations for welfare promotion requires conservation of natural resources, so that the interest of future generation is not sacrificed by excessive exploitation of scarce resources by the present generation. Nature provides enough for mans needs and not his wants/greed. To that extent sustainable development is undermined.

Causes of Air Pollution

Development economists, in recent times have emphasized on acceleration of economic growth for raising per capita incomes of people and industrialization holds the key for rapid growth of the economy. Air pollution is abundant in areas where industries, like petroleum refineries, textiles and pulp and paper are located. Ecological degradation in form of air pollution is the upshot of increasing traffic use, the presence of bad roads, traffic congestion and use of old vehicles and absolute technologies. The existence of slums, badly ventilated houses, smoking cigarette, use of old methods of cooking like wood and coal precipitate air pollution. The use of pesticides by spraying in fields increases the quantity of chemicals used in surrounding atmosphere.

Mining activities involving blasting excavations, crushing and transportation of ore are common these days. Huge quantities of dust become windborne. Thermal power stations use the combustion of coal or petroleum for generation of heat and power, and produce smoke and SO_2 (Sulphar dioxide).

Burning of heaps of solid wastes, diesel generation sets, population growth, air conditioning appliances and construction activities are some of the constellation of factors accounting for air pollution. Reference may be made of Green house effect, which denotes the phenomenon by which the earth's atmosphere traps infrared radiation or heat. Water vapour, CO_2, Methane and Nitrous oxide, no doubt keeps the earth habitable. But, human activities cause mounting concentration of these gases known as chlorofluro carbons (CFCS). Piles of evidence have accumulated in recent years to suggest that global warming has accelerated in the recent past. World glaciers inventory spot lights that, most glaciers around the world have retreated since the turn of the century. It is logical to state that, tropical glaciers and icecaps are sensitive to climate change and may serve as an index to global warming.

It is plausible to believe that atmospheric particulate due to fuel consumption for industrial and heating purposes can scatter and absorb sunlight and may reduce visibility. Among the adverse effects of particulate matter we include corrosion of metals, erosion and soiling of sculptures and buildings.

It follows that agricultural and industrial development sets in motion the tragic drama of ecological degradation. Possible fuel energy policy pursued by several global economies is not environmentally sustainable. It is alarming to note that more than half of words twenty major cities are confronted with air pollution that sets in motion premature deaths and economic losses, There is particulate matter inform of dirt, dust and solid waste that is thrown into the air that is baneful for humans, animals and plants.

Impact of Air Pollution

International standards ensure that there is university of standardization in diverse products and services in the I.S.O. Series. The ISO 9000 part entitled quality management and quality Assurance standards has eleven standards.

Air pollution has hazardous impact on human health. Air pollution is contributory for respiratory disorders in Homo-sapiens. It is common knowledge that, lead particles from vehicles exhaust in higher dose can kill outright but in lower dates may shorten life span of man. Polymer dust, acid fumes mists and solvent vapours in work environment discharges these elements to the outside.

The quality of vegetation is adversely affected by air pollution. Eco-friendly society may is not possible, when farmers make use of chemicals such as insecticides, herbicides and pesticides in agricultures. The pesticides applied in agriculture are likely to produce foliar lesions, chlorosis and reduce fruit sets.

Emissions into the air have repercussions on climate in terms of local rainfall. Of late, environmental economists and public authorities have expressed concern at the adverse impact of emissions in air on ozone layer in atmosphere.

Dust storms pollen grains of flowers are natural sources of air pollution. Air pollution by and large is the by product of human activities. Regardless of the fact that, natural resources are scarce in a country man had exploited scanty natural resources for profit maximization for the present and has discounted there by needs of sustainable development to preserve natural resources for future generations.

Policy Measures

In keeping with the goal of promoting ecological balance in the world, the United Nations General Assembly has declared the International Decade For Natural Disaster Reduction on first January, 1990.

The Air (Prevention and Control of Pollution Act) Act, 1991 has recommended shifting of industries from Urban areas, the obtainment of clearance from State Pollution Control Board for industries which are proposed to be set up and it is binding on the part of industries to follow the air quality measurements as per state/central pollution boards and provide for replacement of pollution generating machinery.

The Centre and State Pollution Central Board advises the government on matters relating to control of air pollution, publishes data on environment pollution and lays down effluent standards. Another weapon to fight the battle of air pollution is the provision of research guidance to pollution control boards both at centre and state levels.

The Motor Vehicles Act, 1939 and the Motor vehicles Act, 1988 covers air pollution generated by automobiles. The state government implements the Act.

Environmental Awareness at Primary school level aims to impart elementary knowledge about environmental issues. Management of natural resource at senior secondary level school seeks to tackle management aspect of natural resources. At college level efforts may be directed to experiment on conservation of natural resources.

Efforts may be made to embark on the path of plantation to abate air pollution. Plan endeavour may strive to discover alternative sources of energy like wind, and solar energy. Another instrument in the tool box of air pollution is pollution check of vehicles. With regard to refined natural gas, it may be stated that use of Compressed Natural Gas (CNG) may be encouraged on massive scale. It can be pleaded that, the use of electric trains may be of much use for commuters from suburban areas and it may reduce local rush in local buses.

Establishment of Automatic traffic control Areas involves reservation of some roads exclusively for automobiles traffic. On the other hand, congested roads and lanes may be declared as automatic traffic central areas.

To combat air pollution, the use of bicycles for local purposes needs a big boost. China has marched on the path.

Above all, environmental impact Assessment should be carried out regularly by scientific personnel and researchers.

It needs recognition, that strict government action be taken against industries, which discharge higher quality of pollutants than prescribed by the state pollution controlling Board. Industries may be shifted from residential areas to industrial areas. Further, use of cow dung and bio-fertilizer may be encouraged in agriculture.

Conclusion

The central conclusion that emerges from the study is that, we should develop a biocentric conscience, that involves a recovery of a sense of kinship between man and nature. The world conference on environment and development commission held in Tokyo on February 27, 1987 has pleaded for a kind of growth with its components of sustainability, equity, Justice and security, sustainable population growth and conservation of the resource base of the world. Some learned bodies like, OECD have suggested that, firms discharging effluents to the environment should be made to pay a price for such discharges related to amount of environmental damage caused. (The polluter pay principle). Luxurious life style may be substituted by simple life style.

Jambeswar has already set in notion the train of Chipko movement in the country. Protection of nature's precious resources is a collective responsibility of one and all, individuals, Government, society, NGO's Youth and Women, and Corporations. The scale of endeavor may be speeded up to create public awareness to protect environment. The *Vedas* declare *"Aum Prudhivi Santhi, Vanaspathi Santi, Apoh Santhi, Sarve Bhabantu Sukhinah"*.

REFERENCES

Several conference volume of Indian Economy Association.

M.L. Jhingan, *Enviromental Economics*, Theory, Practice and Management.

B. Eswar Rao Patnaik, "Sustainable development" *Orissa economic Journal*, 2003.

Index

J

K

L

M

N

O

P